More acclaim for
TUNED TO BASEBALL

"A grand book by a grand guy."

USA Today

"Crisp, clean, hard-hitting . . . Laden with you-heard-it-first anecdotes and genuine good humor."

Baseball Gold

"A unique man, this Ernie Harwell. He can talk baseball and he can write baseball. You'll love his stories of the game."
The Detroit News

"Uplifting, inspirational, humorous. When you're finished, you feel like you do when you've heard Ernie call a game. You realize what a good job he has done."

Baseball Hobby News

TUNED TO BASEBALL

Ernie Harwell

BALLANTINE BOOKS • NEW YORK

Library of Congress Catalog Card Number: 86-2120

ISBN 0-345-36125-3

This edition published by arrangement with Diamond Communications, Inc.

Manufactured in the United States of America

First Ballantine Books Edition: April 1990

To Richard B. Harwell, historian, mint julep expert and brother—the real writer in the family

Special thanks to:

Bill Haney—for his inspiration and his extra effort
on the manuscript.

Jill and Jim Langford—for their advice and direction.

Mary Lynn Wilkins—for her excellent typing.

Lulu Harwell—for getting in the first word
instead of the last.

Chronology: Ernie Harwell.

Born Washington, Georgia January 25, 1918
Atlanta correspondent *The Sporting News* 1934–1948
Sports department *Atlanta Constitution* 1936–1940
Sports director WSB Atlanta 1940–1942
USMC 1942–1946
Atlanta Cracker baseball announcer 1943; 1946–1948
Brooklyn Dodger baseball announcer 1948–1949
New York Giant baseball announcer 1950–1953
Baltimore Oriole baseball announcer 1954–1959
Detroit Tiger baseball announcer 1960–
Inducted into the Baseball Hall of Fame August 2, 1981

Contents

Foreword

IT'S ABOUT TIME.

For the past ten years I've been saying, "Ernie, you should write a book."

"I'm too lazy," has been his answer.

Now with Bill Haney urging him on (plus a little gentle nagging from me) Ernie has recounted some of his experiences as a sportscaster.

I could tell you a lot of things about Ernie Harwell— things he doesn't cover in this book. To know him, you have to go past the chronology in this book and his entry in *Who's Who in America*. You have to live with him for 43 years, share his triumphs and defeats.

I've discovered that the most important values to Ernie are : (1) his relationship to God, (2) his family and (3) his job. Perhaps you'll discern this as you read *Tuned to Baseball*.

Ernie's idea of a roaring good time is relaxing at home with a few close friends and family. There are fifteen of us Harwells including seven grandchildren. Although he loves fine restaurants and a good Broadway show, he'd rather watch his grandchildren put on a singing act with their piping little voices.

Even if he is a stay-at-home, it's a full and exciting

life he shares with you in this book. Yet there are many things he doesn't tell you about himself. I'm proud of him and his accomplishments, so I'll list a few ways you can zero in on my lazy husband.

He is:

(1) Inventor. He holds a U.S. patent on a bottle-can opener and also invented a World Series Fact Wheel.

(2) Actor. Ernie (or his voice) has appeared in *One Flew Over the Cuckoo's Nest, Aunt Mary, Tigertown* and *Paper Lion*.

(3) U.S. Marine. As a writer for the Marine publication, *Leatherneck*, he did a special interview with Mrs. Franklin D. Roosevelt and also covered the recapture of Wake Island. His Wake Island article was included in S. E. Smith's *U.S. Marine Corps In World War II*.

(4) Song Writer. Forty-six of his songs have been recorded. He has collaborated with such song writing greats as Sammy Fain, Johnny Mercer, Jose Feliciano and Mitch Ryder. One of his songs is included in B. J. Thomas' Greatest Hits Album. Other tunes have been recorded by Barbara Lewis, Deon Jackson, Homer & Jethro, Mitch Ryder, Merilee Rush, Tommy Overstreet, Beverly and Duane, and Lee Talboys.

(5) Traveler. He toured Korea, Japan, Iwo Jima and Okinawa on a special trip for the Commissioner of Baseball. Ernie and our family spent a winter in Majorca, Spain, and he has visited many other countries around the world.

(6) Writer. His articles have appeared in *The Saturday Evening Post, Esquire, American Legion, Colliers* and *Reader's Digest*. One of his articles was selected as one of the Best Sports Stories of 1962.

(7) Baseball announcer. He was the first announcer named to the Baseball Hall of Fame while still active in play-by-play.

Also: Ernie was Margaret (GWTW) Mitchell's paper boy in Atlanta, succeeded Marty Marion at second base on the Northside Terrors, shot a hole-in-one, had a racehorse named after him, sang a duet with Pearl Bailey, gave his Christian testimony on a Tampa, Fla. Billy Graham TV special, and was baptized in the Jordan River. That's my Ernie. I hope you enjoy his book.

Lulu Harwell

1

Somehow, They All Manage

FOR THE ONLY FIGHT IN MY BROADCASTING CAREER, I picked a worthy opponent—Leo Durocher.

Leo must have been in hundreds of fights—so many that he probably doesn't remember his skirmish with me. But my fight with Leo is one I certainly won't forget.

Leo was a product of the streets. He left the streets of his childhood only to frequent pool halls or to play ball. He was the consummate competitor.

He was also a great showman. He loved the spotlight and always had to have his court—and his court jester. When I was with the Giants, his court jester was Arch Murray, the baseball reporter of the *New York Post*. But, he was always looking for additional stooges. It was Leo's quest in that direction that triggered our small set-to.

The Giants were coming home by train from Chicago. Russ Hodges and I had finished breakfast and were sitting in my compartment. Russ was relaxing with his cigar. I was reading the newspaper.

Into the compartment breezed Durocher.

"Hi, you guys. What's going on?" he asked.

"Oh, nothing much," answered Russ. "Have a seat, Leo."

I looked up over my paper and said hello.

Before I got an answer, Durocher had smacked his fist into my paper and knocked the pages into my face. I began to boil. Maybe I reacted that way because I had seen how Durocher had picked on Murray and his other stooges. I didn't want to be put down into that class. Usually I am a mild and lazy guy (I was that way long before Steve Martin became a wild and crazy guy) and a little smack of the newspaper wouldn't bother me. This time it did.

Quickly, I jumped to my feet. I grabbed Leo and gave him a bear hug. He struggled to get away.

Meanwhile, Hodges—not wanting to get involved— was serenely sitting back and puffing his cigar.

Leo was mad—fighting back. He grabbed my arm and we fell to the floor of the compartment, both huffing and puffing and not really hurting each other.

As a fight, that one will never make the "Great Fights of the Century" film series. I didn't hurt Leo and he didn't do any damage to me. About all we got out of it was out-of-breath and the realization that we were not ready to go 15 rounds to a finish. Gradually, we both ran out of steam and quit. No hard feelings, no recriminations. I broadcast four years for the Giants and neither of us ever referred to our fight again. I played golf often with Leo, attended parties with him and we got along well.

I believe that Durocher was one of the sharpest managers I ever worked with. I'm sure he slipped later, but in his Dodger and Giant days he was innings ahead of his rivals. He knew the percentages but was not afraid to defy them to play out his hunch. He usually cooperated with his boss-owners, yet would stand up for his own opinions and give full battle to his bosses.

He would lie and cheat; but he was loyal to his friends. And he would do just anything to win. He was impulsive, and—more than anything—he was cunning.

His marriage to Laraine Day was difficult for the American public to understand. Durocher, the gamester from the streets; and Laraine, the sweet-image actress from the Dr. Kildare movies. It didn't make sense. Yet, Laraine could hold her own with her hard business sense and her sometimes tough talk. I always felt that the real manager in that household was not the baseball manager, but the actress. She had Leo pretty much where she wanted him.

Once during spring training in Arizona, Laraine (not too happy with some of Leo's attitudes) began to chide him by calling him "Horseshit" Durocher. Naturally, it was not a term she employed or he enjoyed in public. One night at the dog-track when she had an argument with him over leaving, she walked away from him. A few moments later she had him paged over the PA system at the track.

"Paging H. S. Durocher, paging H. S. Durocher," the public address announcer intoned. Leo didn't keep Laraine waiting long and soon they were on their way home.

The last time I saw him he had another wife, a lovely lady from Chicago. They had come to Hollywood to tape "The Way It Was" show. Bobby Thomson, Ralph Branca, and I—all participants on the show—picked up Mr. and Mrs. Durocher at the Beverly Hills hotel and headed for the studio.

"Frank's opening in Vegas," Leo told us. "Sending his plane for me."

That was only the beginning. From then on, Leo reviewed all of Sinatra's parties, told us of the many gifts Frank had bestowed on him and then switched to Dr. Michael De Bakey, the Houston heart surgeon. Between morsels of information about his heroes and his own comments about aortas, band arrangements, ventricles, and tonal pitch, Durocher instructed the limo driver how to reach the studio—and managed to get us lost.

He was the same old personable Leo, charming all of us all the time. I'm sure that we didn't believe everything he said, but he did make it entertaining.

And he never mentioned the fight that he and I had on that train from Chicago. Neither did I.

The first manager I ever knew was Paul Richards. He managed the Atlanta Crackers when I went to St. Augustine, Florida, to cover spring training for radio station WSB, Atlanta.

That was 1941. I was fresh out of college, sensitive about my youth and inexperience. I bounded up the steps of the creaking old hotel and knocked on Richards's door.

"Come in."

I walked in and found Paul emerging from the bathroom.

"Hi," he said. "When I first saw you I thought you were one of my new ballplayers."

His opener put me at ease. Maybe he sensed somehow that I'd always yearned to be a professional ballplayer. Then, Richards sat down with me and talked about his club, treating me as an equal. He had won me in a hurry.

The first news Paul told me about himself was that he was constipated—a bulletin which wouldn't make the headlines. But it gave me the feeling of being an insider. Throughout his career many of Paul's critics felt he lived in a constant state of constipation. And I'll admit he was caustic, sarcastic, and often bitter. He paid little attention to his players off the field. He was barely tolerant of the media, most of whom considered him aloof. Yet, after a couple of beers he could unbend and without too much urging would recite the second and third stanzas of "The Star Spangled Banner" and President Lincoln's Letter to Mrs. Bixby.

The next morning at breakfast he could be his usual grumpy, silent self. I've sat with him at breakfast in hundreds of coffee shops and often he would never say a single word throughout the entire meal. His friend Jack Dunn, Baltimore Oriole official, used to say: "If Paul drank a bottle of beer at breakfast instead of prune juice, he'd get along a lot better with everybody."

Richards was a master of the put-down and lived by his oft-expressed creed, "I never want to hurt anybody unintentionally." His best zings came while he was golfing. Once I was his partner and having all kinds of trouble with my game. Turning to me with a sardonic half-smile he said: "Ernie, why don't you just go back to the clubhouse and wait 'til I finish the round."

He loved golf. In Baltimore, we'd play 18 holes at the Country Club of Maryland in the morning. Then, he'd rush to the pro shop phone and arrange another game at Five Farms for the afternoon. He designed a special case for his golf clubs (it looked like a midget's coffin) so he could take his clubs on the baseball trips. He even put my name on the case and his bag; but that didn't fool anybody. All who traveled with the team knew about Paul's love affair with the links.

I remember a horrendous schedule he once set up for his Oriole players because he (1) didn't like to fly, and (2) wanted to play golf in Chicago. We had finished a Sunday afternoon game in Kansas City. The next scheduled game was in Baltimore on Tuesday night. I caught a plane after the game and was home by Sunday evening. However, the team didn't leave Kansas City until 11:30 Sunday night. They arrived in Chicago around nine the next morning, then had a layover there until 5:30 Monday night. After wandering around the Loop all day with no hotel rooms, the players hopped the train to Baltimore and arrived home late Tuesday afternoon.

What about Richards? He had his golf. Some cronies met him at the train station. They whisked him away to the golf course where he had a great time until he came back to the train and rejoined his players. During the long ride to Baltimore (needless to say) Mr. Richards didn't discuss his golf game with his train-weary players.

In his younger days Paul walked in his sleep. He once roomed with pitcher Van Lingle Mungo, who had the same problem.

"One night Mungo went sleepwalking," recalled Paul. "He woke up in a closet and made so much noise he woke me up too. I looked around and found myself under the bed.''

Never in his managing career did Richards win a big league pennant. Yet, he earned great respect from his players and coaches. Many players told me, ''He showed me things I never dreamed about.''

Part of his greatness with his players lay in his patience, born of his own long years in the minors.

During World War II, Paul left Atlanta to join the Detroit Tigers. He'd been a catcher and later a manager of the Atlanta team for five or six seasons. But the war had depleted the ranks of the major league teams and he got another chance. I sold an article about him to the *Detroit Free Press* the winter before he reported— the first time my name ever appeared in a Detroit paper.

Paul was 35 years old when he returned to the majors. He stayed with the Tigers four years and then went to Buffalo to become manager of the Tiger farm club there.

The Bison players soon learned how much a perfectionist Richards was. Once he paid an extra electric bill to keep his team working out past midnight. Also, when his Buffalo shortstop had made three errors in the first game of a doubleheader, Richards hustled him out to the infield between games (while the Sunday crowd looked on) and spent the entire intermission rapping grounders to the embarrassed infielder.

Richards had a rule that nobody showered until after he had taken his own shower. Given to brooding over defeats, Paul sometimes sat on a stool in the locker room two hours before showering. His players waited restlessly. They didn't like it, but the trick gave them an extra desire to win.

Some players disliked Paul's methods. Others swore by him. The late Nellie Fox was one of his biggest boosters.

"Paul Richards made a big-leaguer out of me," he told me once. "He used to stay after a game and pitch batting practice to me. He taught me how to hit and how to make the double play. He's the best I ever played for."

Richards was the thinking man's manager. He invented the extra large catcher's mitt for Gus Triandos to handle Hoyt Wilhelm's knuckleball. He sometimes would move his pitcher to first base or outfield, let an infielder pitch to one certain batter and then bring his original pitcher back to the mound. Sometimes, his strategy would involve walking a pitcher with two out to force a fast leadoff man to the plate with a slow runner on first. And then, he came up with a super trick.

The super trick turned out to be too super and not tricky enough. Here was the plan. Richards reasoned that when an opponent tagged at third on a fly and tried to score, the catcher was at a disadvantage on the tag because of his bulky catcher's mitt. So, he instructed his pitcher who backed up the play to exchange his glove for the catcher's mitt during the flight of the ball to the outfield.

Sounds sensible enough, doesn't it?

Only one drawback: When the Orioles tried it, pitcher Bill Wight swapped his left-handed glove to right-handed catcher Joe Ginsberg. The outfielder's throw sailed between Wight and Ginsberg during the exchange. "Back to the drawing board," said Richards.

* * *

Another thinking man's manager was Charlie Dressen. In fact, he and Richards were together on the 1933 Giants when the club won the World Series from Washington. Neither of the deep thinkers got into a game; but the Series did mark the first time that Dressen's brain waves were recognized coast-to-coast.

Charlie had been called up from the Southern League late in the season and appeared in only 16 games for the Giants. He was warming the bench in the fourth game of the Series as the two teams went into the 11th inning tied, 1–1. In the first half of the 11th, the New Yorkers scored a run. But the Senators came back. They filled the bases with one out in their half of the 11th.

Cliff Bolton, a left-hand–hitting catcher, came in to pinch hit for Washington pitcher Jack Russell. The entire Giant infield went into conference. First baseman and manager Bill Terry led the session. The choices: Play in to cut off the run or play back and gamble for the double play to end the game.

All of a sudden, here came Dressen. He had dashed from the Giant dugout and was approaching the brain-busting group on the mound. Terry gave him a quizzical look.

"Hey," said Chuck, "let me tell 'bout this Bolton guy. I played against him in the Southern League. He's real slow. And he hits the ball on the ground. Play back for the double play."

"Okay," said Terry, "we'll try it that way. And Dressen, you'd better be right."

He was right. Bolton grounded to shortstop Ryan. The double play was easy. The Giants won that game and then took the next one and the 1933 World Series.

Not too many bench-warmers would come out in a

World Series and tell the manager how to play the game. But Charlie Dressen had guts and he loved to play the Thinker.

"Hold 'em close and I'll think of something." That was the quote attributed to Charlie in later years. It was often said with a sneer, because many in baseball looked down on the little bantam rooster. However, once you knew him, you appreciated him. Nobody loved baseball more than he. His whole life was wrapped around the game. He was a warm and generous person and, even though his ego stuck out like an umpire's thumb, it never bothered those close to him.

Once in spring training Charlie summoned five of his minor league pitchers from the Tigertown complex in Lakeland to come over to the major league camp and pitch batting practice. After the workout, he dispatched his coach, Frank Skaff, to Dunedin. Skaff returned with five cashmere sweaters for the young pitchers—gifts from Charlie.

If baseball was Dressen's first love, cooking was his second. On team trips from California to Detroit, Charlie always brought bushels of peaches, lettuce, and melons. When he came to your house for dinner he'd say: "I'm the cook now. You relax and let me take over."

Then he'd send everybody scampering for chili peppers, avocados, and other items most housewives don't usually stock.

"I don't worry 'bout how we pitch to the opposition as much as I worry about dropping the paddle while I'm stirring Charlie's chili," coach Stubby Overmire used to say. Indeed, Charlie even cooked in the clubhouse at Tiger Stadium.

While at Detroit Charlie had a utility man named

George Thomas. George was full of pep and good humor, but was miffed because he wasn't playing more.

One afternoon as the game wore into the late innings, George picked up a bat and began to roam up and down in front of Dressen and the other players on the Tiger bench.

He paced from one end of the dugout to the other—anxious to have Charlie send him in at least to pinch-hit.

"George!" yelled Dressen. "Come here."

"Yessir," said Thomas and he briskly walked over to the manager.

"George, I want you to go into the clubhouse right now and stir that chili."

Dressen had an extra warmth for Willie Horton. But he had problems with Willie because Willie wasn't quick in picking up Charlie's signals. In '66 when the Tigers were battling to stay in the race, they were playing a weekend series at Fenway Park against the Red Sox. A very important series with the Yankees starting on Tuesday in New York was next on the schedule.

Before the Saturday game with Boston, Dressen called Horton into his office.

"Willie," he said, "we've got a big series coming up with the Yanks and you're still not getting our signs. You missed another one last night. You know that, don't you?"

"Yessir," said Willie.

"Well," continued Dressen, "this is something very important. You have to know those signs by Tuesday."

Willie scratched his beard, looked up, and asked: "When's Tuesday?"

One of Charlie's closest friends was the concert pianist Eugene Istomin. Certainly the odd couple. A scrapper from the streets and a world-traveled sophisticate who performed for kings and presidents.

"That pie-anna player" was Dressen's term for the pianist. Eugene would suggest trades and strategy and Charlie would listen and make wry comments. Istomin came to spring training with the Tigers and would don a Tiger cap and show up at all the practice sessions.

The last time I saw Charlie I was with Istomin. My wife Lulu and I were invited to a post-concert party at Cranbrook for Eugene, Leonard Rose, and Isaac Stern.

Dressen attended the concert with us. After the performance he and the others went backstage to visit Istomin.

"I'm not feeling good. Upset stomach," Charlie told us. "You go to the party. I'm going home and get some rest."

The next morning he was in the hospital and a week later he was dead.

Before Charlie died, the Tigers were on the road again. We were in Washington when we received the news.

Pat Mullin, Mike Roarke, and I had left the Shoreham Hotel for a golf game with the Washington announcer, Dan Daniel. We had finished the first nine holes at Silver Spring Country Club when one of the assistant pros came out of the pro shop and stopped us on the tenth tee.

"I just heard the news over the radio," he said. "Charlie Dressen died this morning."

It wasn't totally unexpected, but we were stunned. We sat down.

"What shall we do?" I asked. "Don't you think we should go right back to the Shoreham?"

"No," said Pat Mullin. "No sir. Let's go ahead and finish the round. I'm sure that's the way Charlie would like it."

A week later the Tigers honored Dressen with a short pre-game memorial. They asked me to eulogize him. Here is what I said from the field:

"This is a tribute to Charlie Dressen.

And the best possible place to honor Charlie is here at Tiger Stadium.

The baseball diamond was the focal point of Dressen's entire life.

To him, baseball was everything; and Charlie was everything to baseball.

He was a player, a coach, a scout, and a manager. And into each of these jobs, he put his whole heart.

It was here that he belonged.

And it was here that he left his legacy—a legacy of dedication and enthusiasm.

Let us remember Charlie Dressen as a man of dedication and enthusiasm. And let us remember him as a baseball man who loved his game more than life itself."

Another manager you had to like was Jimmy Dykes. I worked with him in both Baltimore and Detroit. Dykes was a wrinkled pixie, a cross between W. C. Fields and Bert Lahr. In fact, he even looked like Lahr. He was warm and friendly, and relaxed. He was the best with the needle since Betsy Ross. Yet, it was always a friendly, gentle needle. He had a lot of friends and they were always around—usually in the clubhouse. Dykes' clubhouse always was filled with kids, too. His was the most relaxed clubhouse I can remember. He had very few rules and prodded his players with a light touch.

He was the Orioles' first manager. He came from the A's to manage at Baltimore in 1954. He also managed the Tigers when I first went there in 1960. It just happened that he managed those two teams during my first season with each of them. And we were together each time for only one year.

Dykes was the only person I knew who chain-smoked cigars. He actually would light one cigar off the previous one. When Jimmy played golf (and he loved the game), he would put about two dozen cigars into his bag and go from there.

When Dykes was fired toward the end of the 1954 season by the Orioles, he gave the shortest announcement I'd ever heard. Clarence Miles, owner of the Orioles, had driven from Boston to Baltimore and announced that he would hold a press conference in his suite at the Kenmore Hotel. All of us media types strolled into the suite. There was Dykes, seated on the sofa, puffing the ubiquitous cigar. He was smiling.

"Hi, Jimmy," said Hugh Trader of the *Baltimore News-Post*. "What goes?"

"I do," answered Dykes.

I know Jimmy was hurting inside but he could find fun even in tragic circumstances.

Mayo Smith couldn't. When Mayo was fired by the Tigers he left with a bitter feeling toward the fans. "They don't know the difference between a major leaguer and a kamikaze pilot" was the way he put it when the fans began to boo the manager who had brought the Tigers a world's championship in 1968.

From their 1968 peak the team dropped to fourth in 1970, 29 games behind Baltimore. And Mayo had to go. I remember running into him in the Tiger parking lot. General Manager Jim Campbell had just fired Mayo in a conference in Jim's office. I walked past Mayo and could tell that he had been crying. It didn't take a genius to know he was fired.

Mayo was conservative with a capital "C." He believed in making out the lineup and letting the players play. That's why his bold move in the 1968 World Series was so startling. He switched center fielder Mickey Stanley to a strange and demanding position, shortstop, in order to get the bat of Al Kaline into the lineup. The move worked. Stanley played a great shortstop and Kaline delivered key hits as the Tigers beat the St. Louis Cards, four games to three, to take the championship.

At the time I thought it was a bad move. I checked about 25 so-called experts on the eve of the Series and they agreed with me. I talked with players, ex-players, scouts, baseball executives, writers, and announcers. Not one of the 25 supported Mayo's strategy. But it worked.

Most baseball historians will remember that move as the keystone of Mayo's managerial career. To me a less significant vignette will stand out in my memory of Smith's career.

One summer afternoon at Tiger Stadium, Willie Horton attempted a diving catch in left field. He dived, missed the ball, and rolled over in obvious pain. When Willie was hurt, it always looked as if he would never play—or even walk again. Usually, his histrionics didn't reflect reality and Horton would stay in the game practically unscathed. But nobody ever knew at the moment of the injury.

This time it looked serious. Horton seemed to be really hurt. As soon as Willie began to writhe on the ground, trainer Bill Behm raced toward him. Manager Mayo Smith was running hard, directly behind Behm. Behm had in earlier years been stricken with polio. He ran toward Willie with a decided limp. Smith, before he could reach the stricken Horton, pulled up lame with a charley horse. He went down on the left-field turf. Behm then had a choice: Attend to the left fielder, or the manager. He chose the manager and Willie had to wait.

It was quite a picture . . . the limping Behm, the suffering Mayo Smith, and Willie Horton agonizing and wondering if anyone would ever pay any attention to him.

Of all the Tiger managers in those early years, I was closest to Bob Scheffing. In fact, he was my broadcast partner after he was fired as manager. His wife Mary was especially close to Lulu and the four of us enjoyed great times together. Bob was the Tiger manager who almost won a pennant.

He managed in 1961 and 1962 and was fired in the middle of the 1963 season. On September 1 of the '61 season, the Tigers were only a game and a half behind the league-leading Yankees. The whole town was excited as we headed for New York. So excited that the Lions, who had a pre-season football game scheduled for Friday night (the same night the Tigers opened at

Yankee Stadium), postponed that game because we were to telecast the Tiger game.

The excitement died quickly. The Yankees won the first game and went on to sweep the series. Before another week had passed, the Detroiters had dropped to ten back and the race was over.

After the Tigers lost those three crucial games to the Yankees, they went to Baltimore. That Sunday night—after the third straight loss—Bob and I ate at the Chesapeake Restaurant. He was staring into his pre-dinner cocktail when a gushy Baltimore matron came over to the table.

"Bob Scheffing," she said, "how could your team do that? The Tigers did the same thing our Orioles did last season. They folded in the stretch. I think that's awful."

Somehow Scheff was able to contain himself. He muttered a few fairly civil words and the lady eventually went back to her table unharmed.

Everybody called Scheffing "Grumpy," but he was far from that. Sometimes he could be blunt, but he was a gracious and generous person. He was a player's manager. They loved him because he was considerate of them. Some people thought he was too good to his players.

Mary shared Bob's concern for his players and their families. One night she got a frantic phone call from Sharyn McLain, the pitcher's new wife.

Sharyn was crying. "I need help," she said. "Denny has left on a road trip. He's left me here alone. I don't have any money or food and I've got this big dog to keep. I don't know what to do."

"Stay there," Mary said. "I'll come get you and you

can stay with me at my house until the team gets back. Don't worry about a thing.''

Bob Scheffing's decency shone through many times during our association. When he first joined me in the radio-TV booths for the 1964 season, there was a conflict concerning the pre- and post-game shows. Bob came to me with his own solution.

''I don't have to work on either show,'' he told me, ''if it would straighten out the situation. Or I'll do either one.''

He was being more than generous because not working either show would mean that I'd be getting an extra $15,000 and he'd be getting nothing.

Eventually we were able to work it out where each of us did a show and received equal amounts. But it was a generous gesture on his part.

There was another episode in Boston in which Bob—in a good-natured way—showed his stubbornness. We were riding on the team bus from the airport to the Kenmore hotel. It was early spring.

''Look,'' said our engineer Howard Stitzel, ''there are some magnolia trees.''

''Those ain't magnolias,'' said Scheffing.

''Oh, yes they are,'' said Stitz.

''I'll bet you. They're not magnolias.''

''Okay,'' said Stitz. ''But if they *are* magnolias, you owe me a brand new baseball.''

We got off the bus and went to a florist next to the hotel. He had a flower book he gave to Stitz. Sure enough, there was a picture of the same tree. It was definitely a Japanese magnolia.

''You owe,'' Stitz told Scheffing and showed him the picture in the book. Bob looked at the picture carefully.

"I'm not paying," he said. "I don't give a damn what the book says. There ain't no way a magnolia is gonna grow in Boston, Massachusetts."

And he never paid Stitzel the baseball.

The most complex of all the managers I have known was Billy Martin. He was an armchair psychologist's dream. Everybody has taken a turn at analyzing Billy and his problems.

Martin came to Detroit to manage the Tigers in 1971. He promptly moved them from a fourth-place finish the year before into second place. Then, in 1972, he led them to the Eastern Division title, losing in the final game of the playoff to an outstanding Oakland team.

Soon, Martin and the Tigers began to sour on each other. Before the 1973 season was over, Billy had been fired.

It was the same pattern that followed Martin wherever he went—Minnesota, Detroit, Texas, New York, and Oakland. Billy is always off to a good start, hailed as the hero by the man-in-the-street, and then somehow attrition sets in. He rubs someone in the front office the wrong way, strife ensues, and Billy Martin walks again.

Vince Desmond, the traveling secretary, was one of the Tiger front office people Billy would sometimes challenge. Martin overruled Desmond one Friday afternoon in New York and almost inflicted a forfeit on the Tigers.

It was raining that Friday afternoon and Martin wanted to delay the departure of the team bus.

"We may not even have to go," he said. "That game might be postponed."

"But Billy," Desmond told him, "Friday is a terrible

day for traffic. And if we don't leave at the usual time, we might get caught in that traffic."

"To hell with it," said Billy. "We'll leave two hours—not three—before the game."

Sure enough, the traffic was heavy. The bus crawled through it, finally getting entangled in the jam of cars and trucks at 125th Street, the middle of Harlem. The pace had been so slow that it was now 7:30. There was no chance the bus would reach Yankee Stadium until after the 8 o'clock starting time.

Martin ran his hands through his hair. He stood up.

"Hey," he shouted to his players, "let's get 12 of you guys off the bus. Get out of here and catch the subway. You'll get there quicker."

The chosen Tigers filed off the bus. A writer or two and Neal K. (Doc) Fenkell, TV director, and his announcer Larry Osterman went with them.

The rest of us stayed on the bus. The bus arrived a few minutes after eight, a couple of minutes before the group which had come on the subway. None of us got to the Stadium before game time. But there was no forfeit—the Yankees didn't want to disappoint the big crowd. They gave the visitors ten minutes of warm-up time and then started the game.

The highlight of the fiasco was a phone call by Doc Fenkell. The TV director had raced to the nearest pay telephone and dialed Yankee Stadium.

"This is Neal Fenkell of the Tigers," he shouted. "We're stuck on the team bus in Harlem and will be late to the game. Don't start the game until the Tigers get there."

A personal charmer when he wants to be, Billy can turn mean and ugly. He can be bitter and vindictive.

He has another quality which has always intrigued me: A tendency to blend into the group personality of his companions. Out with the boys, he can be loud and profane. In quieter, more genteel circles he will be Billy Martin, the gentleman. Always, he is changeable.

Billy is loyal and his friends are loyal to him. They might be critical of him, but they are always loyal. His old pitching coach Art Fowler stuck with him for years; and Billy spent a lot of time and effort to keep Art around him.

All in all, Billy was self-destructive. While he was in Detroit, the going cliché was "Billy Martin's biggest problem is Billy Martin." One night we were waiting in the Minneapolis airport for our Tiger charter plane to take us to Chicago. I was sitting around with Bill Freehan, Al Kaline, Jim Northrup, and Norman Cash. The conversation—as usual—centered on their manager, Billy Martin. Somebody said: "The trouble with Billy is that he's his own worst enemy."

Jim Northrup, who hated Martin even more than the rest, jumped to his feet.

"Not while I'm around, he's not!" he shouted for all the airport to hear.

No matter where he played or where he managed, Billy Martin was always a Yankee. He was forever identified in my mind with Mickey Mantle, Whitey Ford, Hank Bauer, and those other Yankee stars of the 1940s and 1950s. That's the way Billy thinks about himself too. Once a Yankee, always a Yankee.

Another Tiger manager who was identified with the Yankee dynasty was Ralph Houk. What a start he had as a manager. He began his big league managing career with the Yankees in 1961, breezing to a pennant with 109 victories. His Yankees also won for the next two years. After that Houk never won a title.

At Detroit, he was saddled with mediocre teams and in five years never finished higher than fifth.

Ralph had one quality he needed in Detroit— patience. He sat back and didn't hurry the youngsters the Tiger farm system had provided. He let Alan Trammell and Lou Whitaker and the others develop at their own pace. When the Tigers celebrated their 1984 World's title they had to look back to the mid-'70s and thank Ralph Houk for his patience.

Before I knew Ralph, I didn't realize what a patient manager he was. I had heard stories of his temper. I had heard about the old tough Army major who had risen from the rank of private . . . how he saw action at Bastogne and the Bulge and won the Silver Star, Bronze Star, and Purple Heart. Recountings of some of his baseball fights were numerous. In other words, he was one tough guy.

I found him different. Pleasant, but firm. He sat and watched. But when he was riled, his temper exploded. He loved to kid and needle, but he was never vicious. On the road he was a loner. He was one of the few managers who almost never went out with his coaches or the media for an evening meal. Most of the time he would stay in his room, alone.

"What does he do all that time, alone in his room?" I asked one of the Tiger coaches.

"He works on the lineup. He likes to fool around with different batting orders," was the answer.

Ralph's bright spot in Detroit was Mark (the Bird) Fidrych. Even after Mark's arm was gone and the Tigers

had given up on him, it was Houk, then managing the
Red Sox, who gave him his final chance. Ralph liked
the Bird for the same reason most of us did—he was
ready for a fresh, new baseball personality, a youngster
who simply wanted to play and didn't worry about how
big a salary he could make or how many headlines he
might be able to achieve.

The year before the "Year of the Bird" was a low
point in Tiger history. Houk's patience saw it through.
In 1975, for the second straight year the team finished
last, this time losing 102 games. They once dropped 19
straight games. That losing streak ended August 16 at
Anaheim when Ray Bare shut out the Angels. One LA
writer put it this way: "The Tigers had a chance to tie
the American League record last night, but they choked
and beat the Angels, 8-0."

The Tigers were never that bad again. In 1978 Houk
had pushed them over .500 for the first time as a Tiger
manager. After that season he decided to retire. He
spent the next two years in Florida, golfing, fishing, and
taking life easy.

"I found out you can play only so many rounds of
golf and take only so many fishing trips. That's why I
came back," Ralph explained when he returned to
manage the Red Sox. He's retired again now and the
baseball world wonders if he'll ever come back again.
It will be a shame if he doesn't.

After Houk, the Tigers went to their farm system and
gave the 1979 manager's job to Les Moss, a quiet, unassuming career man. Les seemed awed by the Tiger
stars and the media. In June, Jim Campbell moved

quickly. He sacrificed Moss to sign George (Sparky) Anderson as the new Detroit manager.

Jim couldn't wait.

"I knew if I didn't persuade Sparky then and there, some other club would grab him. He had several offers before I got to him," Jim explained.

When Anderson reported, he guaranteed the Tiger fans a winner within five years. And five years later he delivered that winner. The 1984 Tigers raced to a 35-5 start, repulsed every opposition move and won the Eastern Division by 15 games over second-place Toronto. They swept the playoff series with Kansas City and then trounced San Diego in the World Series, four games to one.

Sparky became the first manager in history to win over 100 games for two different teams. He also became the first manager to win a World Series for an American League and a National League team.

Sparky Anderson is the best of all the managers I have known. Not only because of that great record, but because he is an outstanding human being.

He loves his work but he loves people even more. He is personable and polite and he is always available. He can walk with the common man, but he is at ease with the top men in industry and government.

In the summer of 1984, Jim Campbell took Sparky, Al Kaline, George Kell, and me on a tour of the New York Stock Exchange. Sparky attracted more attention that summer morning than Eastman-Kodak or IBM. I wouldn't say the world economy stood still, but there was a large group of brokers and others crowding around Anderson to get his autograph.

"Go get 'em, Sparky."

"How 'bout those Tigers."

"Love you, Sparky."

Those were some of the cries directed toward the Tiger manager.

On our morning walks, it was the same routine. Some young secretary would stop Sparky for his autograph. Or a janitor would come up to him just to say hello.

He can't escape. That silver-gray mop and that rugged, wrinkled face is one of the most recognizable in America.

He is always willing to stop and spend time with these fans. When he gives his autograph, he thanks them. There is a true love affair between Sparky and America.

Why? I think it's because these people can discern the humanness of Sparky. Somehow that quality shines through to all of them.

For instance, when Anderson first came to the Tigers, he had to make a choice about his coaching staff. The quality of his character can be told by the way he faced that problem. This example involved two of Sparky's best friends.

One was George Scherger, Sparky's first manager when Anderson began his professional career at Santa Barbara in 1953. The other was Billy Consolo, who grew up with Sparky and played sandlot and high school baseball with him.

For his coaching staff at Detroit, Sparky hired his friend Billy Consolo. He almost hired his friend George Scherger, but didn't.

It was a tough selection for the new Tiger manager. Fired by Cincinnati, Sparky was spending the early summer of 1979 away from baseball. It was the first time in 29 years he had been home during baseball season. He was playing golf one afternoon with Consolo and thinking over various offers to manage.

"Billy," he told his friend, "when I manage again, I want you to coach for me. You know the game and you're highly qualified. I can sure use you."

"I'm ready," Consolo told him. "Just call me."

Consolo had been out of baseball for 16 years, but he was a close friend. And, if anybody needs a friend, it's a big league manager.

"You've got to have somebody close by to talk with," Anderson says. "You have to have a friend to confide in. There's so much pressure day-to-day in this job."

Sparky accepted the Detroit managing job in mid-season of 1979 and Billy Consolo came with him as his coach. Now Sparky had to fill in the ranks of his coaching staff for 1980, his first full season. He kept Gates Brown from the previous regime. He hired Alex Grammas, who had been his third base coach at Cincinnati.

He called Roger Craig, the deposed San Diego manager, and hired him as pitching coach. Then there was Dick Tracewski, who like Gates Brown was a member of the old coaching staff.

After Anderson took over the Tigers in mid-season of 1979, he contacted George Scherger.

"I wanted him," Sparky recalled. "He is one of the smartest baseball men I'd ever known. Also, one of my closest friends. He was a man I knew I could depend on."

Sparky offered him a coaching job. Scherger said he'd come to Detroit the next season. It was set.

As the season rolled along, Anderson observed the work of Dick Tracewski—the way he handled himself, the way he related to the players, the way he studied and knew the opposition. He was impressed. So much so that he wanted to keep Dick.

But on next year's staff there was room for only one more coach. The choice had to be made between George Scherger, Sparky's close friend, and Dick Tracewski, a man he knew fitted the job better than anyone else.

Sparky made his choice. He took Tracewski.

He phoned Scherger and explained. "I'm not backing down," he told him, "but you're my friend. You've been a manager and you know what Tracewski can mean to me and this team."

"I understand," Scherger told him.

Scherger and Anderson are still very close friends. Scherger continues to work in the Cincinnati organization as a Red coach. He is highly respected throughout baseball. But he's not a Tiger coach because Sparky had to choose a man he thought better fitted the role.

Sparky's best friends: Billy Consolo and George Scherger. Billy got a job with Sparky; Scherger didn't. And Anderson knows that he had made the right choice. With that choice he built an outstanding coaching staff.

In Anderson's first season, he faced some rough going. Some of the fans didn't approve of the way he spoke out and made bold predictions. He became a target for some of the "boo birds" at Tiger Stadium.

Sparky himself felt that he made a mistake in taking the job. He had been the new Tiger manager less than two weeks when he called his wife Carol in Thousand Oaks. "Honey," he told her, "we've got a bad team. I've never seen a bunch so unprofessional. They just come to the park and they seem satisfied to finish fourth or fifth."

Later Sparky exploded in a clubhouse meeting and told his players how he felt.

"You're a bunch of frauds. How can you put on a uniform and call yourselves major leaguers," he demanded. "I can't tolerate this losing and I'm going to have a winner. I'll have one, if I have to trade every player in this room."

He did trade many of them. He released others. He put together the pieces of the puzzle until he completed the picture he wanted—his kind of team. In '84 they went out and won everything for him.

But there was doubt in Detroit. Sparky took a ribbing, too. The fans kidded him mostly about his promises and predictions. I'll admit I gave him a little jab, too. I was really fond of the guy from the first time we met. But that didn't keep me from needling him. Here is a little banquet skit I did about Sparky in January, 1983—just prior to his fourth full year as Tiger manager:

This is a Tiger low-light presentation.

Not a motion picture . . . The Tigers haven't been in motion since 1972 . . . It's a slide presentation. Nothing new, the Tigers have been on a slide for the past ten years. . . .

So, let's look at our slides. . . .

June, 1979, Kalamazoo . . . John Fetzer in his office, thinking about firing Les Moss as Tiger manager . . . Fetzer is reading his copy of *Rolling Stones*—gathering no Moss.

Next slide: Fetzer, humming "I need a gal in Kalamazoo" . . . phones Jim Campbell. Fetzer says, "Jim, fire Moss . . . Get that Loni Anderson from

Cincinnati. If Moss can't win with Dan Gonzales, Ed Putman, Dave Machemer and Sheldon Burnside, he can't win with anybody . . . I want to see Les of Moss and More of Loni.''

Next slide: An excited Campbell is phoning Sparky Anderson . . . Jim was too excited to realize that Fetzer wanted *Loni* Anderson.

Next slide: Background on Sparky . . . Real name *George* . . . Little George, six years old, is being vaccinated for school . . . They're using what was then called a Victrola needle.

Next slide: George's mother talking to George . . . ''All you want to do, George, is play baseball. How will you ever make it in this cruel world?'' George answers, ''I'll manage.''

Next slide: George attending Casey Stengel University of the King's English . . . The Dean (Dizzy Dean) is talking . . . ''George, I want you to major in the care and treatment of language fractures . . . Think you can handle it?'' George says: ''I'll manage.''

Next slide: 1959 . . . Sparky now playing with the Phillies . . . His manager, Eddie Sawyer, says: ''George, how you gonna stay in baseball? There's no place for a .218 hitter.'' George says: ''I'll manage.''

Next slide: Sparky at Cincinnati . . . He's won only four National League pennants, but the GM Dick Wagner is writing his own Wagnerian opera . . . And he's giving Sparky the aria. Dick says: ''Hate to do this, Sparky, but you're fired.'' Sparky says: ''I'll manage.''

So, Sparky comes to Detroit . . . Fetzer thought he

was getting Loni Anderson, Jim Campbell settled for Sparky Anderson . . . And a lot of the fans and media who have heard Sparky's fairy tales are beginning to believe the Tigers got Hans Christian Anderson.

Next slide: Spring training, 1983 . . . Sparky's office in Lakeland . . . Tom Gage, Brian Bragg, Vern Plagenhoef, the beat writers, . . . are with Sparky?'' . . .

Sparky says: ''You guys aren't qualified to write baseball. How do you think you can cover my team for a whole season?'' . . .

They all answer in unison: ''We'll manage.''

Final slide: Sparky on phone with Campbell . . . He says: ''These writers think they can manage my club . . . What shall I do?''

Campbell says: Go to the bar . . . buy them all Sparky Anderson cocktails . . . They'll never bother you again.'' . . .

Sparky says: ''What's a Sparky Anderson cocktail?'' . . .

Jim answers: ''A Sparky Anderson cocktail? Three of them and you can't manage anything all summer long.''

That summer Sparky did manage his Tigers into second place. By the next January, he had the feeling they could win it all in 1984. He was right.

He and I became very close during the '84 season. I'd walk with him almost every morning when the team was on the road. We'd walk for an hour and Sparky would talk. I talked too, but listened the majority of the time.

Most of all I learned that Sparky Anderson is a master psychologist. He had to light a fire under some of the Tigers. He had to stroke others. Sometimes he goaded them, sometimes cajoled and sometimes babied them. Jack Morris was a problem for a while with his silent sulk. Sparky talked him out of not talking. And when the playoffs rolled around, Jack came into Anderson's office and told him, "Pitch whoever you want in the first playoff game and I'll understand."

There was a mid-season flap about Lou Whitaker not wanting to go to the All-Star game. Sparky stroked him.

"Lou," he told his second baseman, "you are an outstanding player. I know that your fans expect you to play in that All-Star game. I'm not telling you that you have to go, but I'm sure your fans expect it of you."

No problem. Lou Whitaker went to the All-Star game.

When Alan Trammell was becoming inundated in early June with too much attention from the media, Sparky stepped in. He told Alan not to make any more outside appearances which would take away from his concentration on the game. Anderson also acquiesced when Kirk Gibson asked him not to talk about his great potential.

"That was one of my hardest jobs," Sparky admits, "but I think it helped to keep the pressure off Gibson."

Anderson rides high when his team wins. A loss will send him into a funk. His coaches are constantly making an effort to level out his emotional ride.

His coaches and his players respect him. They understand what kind of a person he is. They know that Sparky is always thinking about the other person.

The coaches who are especially close to Sparky know

about this quality. Maybe some of the players he has managed haven't discerned it. But I know one who has. He's Pat Corrales, the Cleveland Indians' manager.

In 1970 Sparky was the rookie manager of the Cincinnati Reds. The Reds won the pennant that year and met Baltimore in the World Series. Corrales was Sparky's second string catcher (not too many guys were going to beat out Johnny Bench). Pat was in his third year of hanging on with the Reds. It was also the 14th year in Pat's undistinguished playing career.

The Orioles were too strong for the Reds in that Series and beat them four games to one. In the final game at Baltimore, the Orioles were leading 9–3 in the ninth. It was all over—just a matter of three more outs.

Johnny Bench led off the ninth against Baltimore's Mike Cuellar and lined to Brooks Robinson at third. Lee May struck out. One to go and the Orioles were champions.

Pat Corrales was watching the action from the bench. He had not appeared in the Series. It was his first Series and likely his last. Manager Anderson looked down the bench toward Corrales.

"Pat," he told him, "get up there and hit for Hal McRae. You deserve to be in a World Series and this might be your only chance."

Pat batted for McRae, grounded to Brooks Robinson at third, and the Series was over. But he had been to bat in a World Series—thanks to a thoughtful manager.

2

Mileposts of The Season

BASEBALL HAS ITS OWN CALENDAR—THE SCHED-ule. All of us with even the remotest connection with the game live and die by the schedule. It enables me to dodge speaking engagements: "Oh, I'm sorry, but I'll be out of town on May 16, otherwise I'd be happy to speak to your sales group." Yet, it enables others always to locate me. Using the schedule, any deputy sheriff will know that I'm with the Tigers for that night game in Milwaukee on July 23.

Between opening day and the World Series there are markers along the way—Memorial Day, Fourth of July, the All-Star game and the playoffs. Some of these have existed forever; other markers are new.

When I reached the majors in 1948, Memorial Day loomed much larger on the schedule than it does now. It was the first check point in a team's progress. Also, it meant doubleheaders for everybody—usually day doubleheaders. The Fourth of July has also lost some of its significance. It has been replaced by the All-Star game. Before the All-Star game became such an important extravaganza, the media made big noises about the Fourth of July. The established wisdom was that the leaders of each league on the Fourth would meet in the World Series. Stories and analyses laced the nation's papers about that theory. It was as inevitable as the Christmas story about a tree display or the New Year's item concerning the first baby born in the new year.

Now, it's the All-Star time when we all stop and reflect. Even the stats are divided into two parts, the year before and after the All-Star game. All-Star time and the Fourth of July aren't many days apart, so, it really doesn't make a great deal of difference.

Labor Day used to be another measuring point in the baseball schedule. It meant a month to go. And it was—and still is—a time to confess that maybe your team wouldn't go anywhere but home and that you'd have to look to the inevitable next year. Now, although Labor Day still means something on the calendar, baseball is pointing toward the playoffs.

Playoffs are big. They mean either you win or you're forgotten. There is more tension in the playoffs than in the World Series. Three out of five victories is the prize and the whole series can be over quickly.

In the World Series the pace is more leisurely. A team has room—not much, but some—for a loss or two. It can still come back. But the World Series is the darling of the media. That's when writers, broadcasters, and others converge on the scene and magnify every bit of action on or off the field.

My favorite times of the year are two: The World Series and opening day.

On opening day, you start out fresh. Spring training is over. Everybody is even.

It's a real happening in some cities and just the first game of the season in others. In Detroit, opening day is a civic, social, and sporting event. The whole town turns out. The event dominates the air waves and the newspapers. Not only is the sports section jammed with Tiger type, the family sections and the society pages also have pictures and text with a baseball connection.

Opening day in Detroit is to baseball what Easter is to the church. The faithful come out, but a lot of the once-a-year attendees are there too.

Several years ago when Rick Ferrell was a Tiger GM, a close friend of his (one who knew little about baseball) ran into Rick as the stands were emptying after an opening day loss.

"Tough luck, Rick," he told the Tiger GM. "But we'll get 'em next year."

My own opening day memories go back to my boyhood days at Ponce de Leon Park when the Atlanta Crackers in those baggy pinstriped whites marched to the flag pole to the cadence of a military band. The mayor was always there to toss out the first ball. And the fire department presented the manager with the ubiquitous floral horseshoe.

Years later, after I had been overseas with the Marines, one particular opening day became one of the most important days in my broadcasting career. That opening day—1946—was the day that decided for me that I would be a baseball announcer.

I had enlisted in July 1942, gone to Marine boot camp at Parris Island, South Carolina. Afterwards I was stationed in Atlanta on a public relations assignment.

When the 1943 baseball season rolled around, I was still in Atlanta. And the Atlanta Crackers were in need of an announcer.

Cracker owner Earl Mann, who had known me from my radio work on WSB and as a *Sporting News* writer, asked me to broadcast the games.

"I'll do it, Earl," I told him, "as long as I'm stationed here. But I won't keep the money. Turn my check over to the Red Cross."

It was agreed. I began to broadcast baseball for the first time. However, my career was soon cut short by the Marine brass.

"Harwell," the Major told me, "there's been criticism from civilians. They don't think it's correct for a man to be broadcasting a baseball game while he is in the Marines. You'll have to stop."

I expressed my regrets to Earl Mann and he understood.

"However," he told me, "I like the way you broadcast. When you get out of the service, Ernie, I want you to be my announcer full-time."

I was sent back to line duty in the Marines and forgot about baseball. In January, 1946, I came back from overseas, was discharged, and headed home to Atlanta.

The next few months were crucial to my career. My sports announcing job at WSB was waiting for me, but the station had no room for full-time sports programming because of its commitments to NBC. I decided to free-lance, putting all my hopes on one job—the Cracker broadcasting spot.

"I remember the promise," Earl Mann told me. "And I want you to broadcast our games, but I'm having a real battle with Radio Station WATL. They have bought the rights and sold the games to Wheaties. WATL is insisting that their sports director, Stan Raymond, be the announcer.''

I could understand that. Stan was a friend of mine. I couldn't blame him. Also, the station could save money by using one of its staff. Wheaties was a new sponsor and probably would follow the dictates of WATL.

"Don't forget me," I urged Mann.

"I won't," he assured me.

I left town for a tour of military hospitals for *The Sporting News*, showing movies and talking to servicemen. Also, that spring I broadcast the Masters golf tournament on NBC. When I returned from the Masters, time was getting short. Mann was still putting up a battle for me. But the radio station would not budge. They insisted on their man, Stan Raymond.

With opening day at Ponce de Leon Park only a week away, I phoned Mann.

"Nothing's settled yet," he told me. "The station still won't give in."

I waited. No word. Two more days passed. Still, no word.

"Maybe I did the wrong thing," I told my wife, Lulu. "I should have stuck with WSB and forgotten about free-lancing and the Cracker job."

"Don't give up," she said.

I hadn't given up but panic was beginning to creep into my psyche.

It was now the day before the opener. Mann and WATL were still at odds, each side holding out. WATL for Raymond, Mann for me.

I hardly slept all night long. At breakfast I told Lulu

I didn't have a chance. Still, I waited at the phone—just in case.

At 10:15 the phone rang. It was Earl Mann.

"Ernie," he shouted, "I won. I held out. I insisted on you. They finally came across. Come on out to the park. You're my announcer and you're working this afternoon."

That was my start as a baseball announcer. Without Earl Mann, I wouldn't have even started. I don't think any other baseball executive would have stood up for his choice with such strong loyalty. The easy way would have been to go along with the station. Earl Mann didn't take the easy way. He wanted me and he stood by me.

In 1981 when I was to be enshrined at Cooperstown, I phoned Earl Mann and thanked him for that stand. I invited him to join my family and me at the August ceremonies. Illness prevented him from making the trip and I missed having him there with the people who mattered so much to me.

Believe me, he mattered. If not for Earl Mann, my baseball announcing career would never have started.

Yes, that was my first opening day as a play-by-play man.

The openers in Brooklyn and at the Polo Grounds weren't really special.

New York seemed to swallow up the festive ceremonies and other days that followed in those Dodger and Giant seasons seemed larger in importance than the openers. Baltimore was different. The first opener there in 1954 was an outstanding event. Big league baseball was coming back to Baltimore for the first time since the American League season of 1902. And I was the first Oriole announcer in major league history.

The team split its first two games in Detroit and caught the train for Baltimore. We arrived the morning of the opener. The players put on their uniforms before they reached the railroad station.

They hopped off the train and paraded through the streets of the city.

When we reached Memorial Stadium, workmen were putting finishing touches on the stadium. A misty rain threatened postponement. The Orioles didn't disappoint the capacity crowd. They beat Paul Richards's White Sox, 3–1. Clint Courtney and Junior Stephens hit home runs and the O's began their stay in Baltimore on a happy note.

In my six years at Baltimore no other opener was as important or as festive as that first one. Some weren't even sell-outs.

In 1960 I experienced my first opener as a Tiger announcer. But before we went to Tiger Stadium that year, the Detroiters opened in Cleveland. It was one of the coldest days I would ever experience. The chilling wind blew off the lake at George Kell and me. The two teams battled for 15 innings and four hours and 54 minutes before the Tigers beat the Indians, 4–2. My thoughts were mainly on not freezing and getting back to the hotel where I might thaw out.

The game was exciting. It marked the first time for Rocky Colavito as a Tiger and for Harvey Kuenn as an Indian. They had been traded for each other on the final day of spring training. Colavito, the home run champion, for Kuenn, the batting champion.

The Tigers opened a couple of days later at home. By then the weather had changed and they played the White Sox in 80-degree temperature before a packed house. My most vivid memory about that opener is that of the late Nellie Fox and his consummate kindness under adverse circumstances.

Opening day at home always is marked by complete confusion. It's the first day in the park. Everybody wants everything done that day. Nobody knows where anything is. And there are always people around who really don't belong there and show up only once a year. Also, it's a time when nothing mechanical ever seems to work.

All these factors merged into our opener.

George Kell and I were working together, broadcasting on both radio and TV. We conducted a pre-game interview show and our choice was Nellie Fox. We did the 15-minute chat with Nellie. Everything went great. After we finished, the director said, "Sorry, guys, we had some trouble with the camera. We'll have to do it again."

By then, Nellie had gone back to the field for practice. I had to go get him and ask him to re-do the interview. He agreed. Again, all was well. Again, the director said: "Something's wrong with the tape. Some streaking on it. It won't go."

Again, I found Fox. And he agreed to re-tape.

This time it took. But only because of Fox's kindness that afternoon did we ever get on the air with the interview.

It was at the start of that season that Kell and I had another goofy taping experience. The team was off to a good start, winning the first five games. In those days, before we went on the road our TV interviews had to be taped for later airing. (Live TV interviews were not possible for road games.) George and I decided to interview Tiger catcher Lou Berberet.

Our tape interview went this way:

"Well, Lou, how do you feel about the Tigers?"

"Terrific. If we can just keep going this way, everything will be beautiful."

All of which sounded fine at the time. The only problem was that as soon as we made the tape, the Tigers lost the next ten games. And when the interview aired, they were in the midst of that losing streak and Berberet was saying, "Terrific. If we can just keep going this way, everything will be beautiful."

Another zany opening-day episode happened to me as a magazine writer. I had written the cover story for *Parade* magazine about the U.S. presidents and their tradition of throwing out the first ball of the season.

My lead read: "Thirty-three million people selected the pitcher who'll start the 1953 baseball opener at Washington on Monday, April 13. This time they picked a real pro—a right-hander named Dwight Eisenhower who is the only presidential first ball tosser ever to play professional baseball."

Before scheduling the article, the editors of *Parade* checked with the White House and were assured the President would throw out the first pitch. Then Eisenhower decided he didn't want to attend the opener. He planned instead to go to Augusta for the Masters' golf tournament.

When *Parade* editor Jess Gorkin heard this, he phoned me.

"What about Ike going to Augusta?" he asked. "Our issue is already printed. We've got him tossing out the first ball. Do you think he'd change his mind and attend the opening baseball game?"

How was I to know? I was just a guy who wrote the story.

"We've checked our man in Washington, Jack Anderson," Gorkin continued, "but Ike still says he's going to the Masters. Can you phone Clark Griffith, the Senators' owner? I understand he's close to the President. Maybe he can convince him to come to the game."

I phoned Griff. He told me he'd try. I'm sure he did; but the President remained firm and went to Augusta.

Unable to change Ike's mind, *Parade* then sent out a short bulletin to all their papers. The papers ran a correction item on page one, saying that President Eisenhower was not going to toss out the first ball, but would be in Augusta instead.

Ike went to Augusta and enjoyed the Masters. Ironically, the opening day game in Washington was postponed because of rain and on Thursday, April 16, the President tossed out the opening pitch anyhow.

If opening day gets baseball off to a smash start, it's the World Series which always provides a fitting climax to every season. I don't know which event is my favorite. It's probably the World Series because I experience that thrill in a personal way only rarely.

The first World Series I remember happened when I was eight years old. It was one of the classics. I listened on a crystal set in the basement of our home in Atlanta. In the seventh game of that 1926 Series, Grover Cleveland Alexander came out of the St. Louis bullpen and fanned the Yankees' Tony Lazzeri in the climactic moment.

From then on I was hooked. Since 1926, I have either heard or seen every World Series except the 1945 Series. I was with the Marines in China. We tried to get the games on Armed Forces radio, but never were able to hear them.

The first Series I saw in person was in 1935. My

uncle, Lauren Foreman, lived in Evanston, Illinois. He invited me to come to Chicago to see the Tigers play the Cubs. Prior to that I'd seen only one big league game. The weather was bitter cold. Uncle Lauren didn't care for baseball, so he stayed home and one of his friends took me to the games.

Almost 30 years later, I was a World Series broadcaster. Nothing in our business matches that assignment. I had dreamed about it for years. Finally in 1963, after 15 years of big league broadcasting, I worked on the Yankee-Dodger series.

"You'll be paid on a per game basis," NBC told me. "So you'd better hope that the Series goes a full seven games."

What happened? The Dodgers swept the Yankees in four games.

My partner was Joe Garagiola. We worked the radio together. I almost didn't work.

I had waited 15 years for this chance and I almost blew it. During the last two weeks of the season I came down with a cold and a sore throat. I managed to croak my way through the final games of the Tiger schedule, but I felt weak.

The Series opened at Yankee Stadium and I reported to NBC the afternoon before the first game. I said nothing about my condition and nobody detected my illness.

That night I couldn't sleep. Anticipation, nervousness, and my run-down condition combined to keep me tossing and turning in my bed at the Roosevelt hotel. My nose was running. I was hot with fever and I began to worry about missing the whole Series.

"Here I am," I told myself, "after all this waiting.

And tomorrow I'm not going to broadcast because of this fever. I'll have to tell NBC to get somebody else.''

I still couldn't sleep. I'd been taking aspirin, but nothing else. I got up at 2:30 a.m., dressed, and headed out on the streets of Manhattan, looking for a drugstore. I wandered through the streets and finally located an all-night pharmacy on Lexington Avenue. The druggist sold me cough medicine and sleeping pills.

On my way back to the hotel I saw an old friend of mine, Harry Caray, then a Cardinal announcer. Harry was probably the only radio guy besides me who was exploring the streets of New York at such an hour.

The medicines worked. I slept a little late that morning, but crawled out of bed and made it to Yankee Stadium.

The broadcast went well. I was still aching and my voice wasn't what I would have liked for it to be, but Joe and I did the job and were on our way.

I enjoyed working with Garagiola. However, at Dodger Stadium in Los Angeles there was a strange reaction.

One of the newsmen came to me and said: ''I heard you guys broadcasting the game on the PA this afternoon.''

''No,'' I told him. ''What you heard was the sound of our voices coming from transistor radios all around the stadium.''

Because many fans had brought their radios to the games, it did create a sound similar to the public address system. I noticed while we were working that if Garagiola would tell a joke, a wave of laughter would roll through the stadium. People were reacting to the radio broadcast instead of reacting to what was happening on the field.

That '63 Series was the one in which Mel Allen lost his voice in the seventh inning of the fourth (and final) game. Vin Scully, who was working with him, had to take over for the rest of the game.

Mel's voice problems had began to touch him late in the summer of 1963. His doctor prescribed rest, but Mel refused to rest. He was a constant talker. He loved to talk and argue about baseball. His partner, Red Barber, and others begged him to slow down. The climax came when his voice gave out in the final World Series game.

In the seventh inning Mickey Mantle smashed a home run to tie the game, 1–1. Shouting above the roar of the crowd, Allen lost his voice. He motioned to Scully and Vin took over the mike. Allen headed for the press box for lemon and hot coffee to clear the voice. By the time he could speak clearly again, the game was over. The Dodgers had won, 2–1, to sweep the Series.

It was the last Series for Mel. He had broadcast a total of 19, beginning in 1938. No other announcer was more identified with World Series' broadcasts than Mel Allen.

Allen's booth was next to mine. I looked over at him and empathized with him.

"There's Mel," I told myself. "He's the most celebrated baseball announcer of our day. He's sitting there unable to work on the most prestigious of all jobs in our profession—all because the same affliction which I was lucky enough to overcome has devastated him."

It was a sad moment as I watched Mel knocked out of his last Series at the crucial moment in that final game. Never again did he broadcast a World Series game. And, in less than a year, he had been fired by the Yankees.

I didn't work another World Series until 1968 when

the Tigers met the Cardinals. I worked that year with Pee Wee Reese on NBC radio, broadcasting the games in St. Louis. George Kell worked with Curt Gowdy on TV, doing the games in Detroit. This time I didn't feel as nervous as I had in 1963. The tension was there, but I felt more at ease because my team was in this Series. I was surrounded by friends.

But this Series was also much more emotional for me than the first one because my team and my friends were involved. When the Tigers played badly I was embarrassed. Their loss in the fourth game in Detroit was the most embarrassing. This game was delayed by rain for 74 minutes and soon became a farce.

Playing in a misty rain, the Cards established a 6–0 lead by the fifth inning. They wanted to hurry up the game to make it official. The Tigers began to stall. Tiger players sloshed around while Cardinals attempted to make outs deliberately. And it continued to rain. Finally the umps called on the two managers, the Tigers' Mayo Smith and the Cards' Red Schoendienst, to quit the antics. The Cards humiliated the Tigers, 10–1, and led the Series with 3 wins to 1.

That Sunday was my longest day in baseball. Emmet Tracy and other friends were to stage a party in my honor that night at the Mauna Loa restaurant. Many of the radio, TV and press had been invited. As the game dragged on, I knew that most of them would miss the party because of the delay which would bring them right up to their deadlines. Also, everyone felt so terrible about the way the Tigers were performing.

"That party will be a bust," I told Lulu. "I don't think anybody will show."

I was wrong. A few newspaper men missed it, but a

mob of other people jammed the classy new Mauna Loa. Doug Jacobs's Red Garter Band was there. A lot of people from the music world (including my close friend Ollie McLaughlin and his wife Ruth) showed up. Also Tom Harmon, John DeLorean, Kelly Harmon, Bob Fenton, publisher Roger Stanton, J. P. McCarthy, and many others made it a great party.

Yet, I suppose most of us will never forget that long, rainy dreary afternoon at Tiger Stadium and the Tigers' humiliating loss.

They came back, won the next day and then went on to take the final two games and win the Series.

Jim Northrup hit a two-run triple in the seventh inning of the final game to break up a scoreless pitching duel between Mickey Lolich and Bob Gibson. That was the key blow of the Series and my big moment on the air.

In the eighth inning I headed for the clubhouse and Jim Simpson took over for me at the NBC mike. When the victorious Tigers raced into their clubhouse I was there to interview them on both NBC TV and radio. It was a wild and joyous celebration.

In '84 they did it again. This time the Tigers jumped ahead with 35 wins in the first 40 games of the season. They met every challenge. They won their Eastern Division, then swept Kansas City in three games in the playoffs for the American League pennant.

This was a different World Series experience for me. The new baseball TV-radio contract allowed our own local station, WJR, Detroit, to do its own broadcast. Paul Carey and I were able to continue with our broadcasts throughout the Series.

It was a bittersweet kind of time for me. My team, the Tigers, had made the Series. All of Detroit and

Michigan (plus Tiger fans all over the world) were ecstatic. The Tigers not only were a team with outstanding talent, they were also a team made up of some top-notch people. The players had a feeling for each other. They were a team in the true sense of the word.

Yet, my euphoria was tempered by the illness of Paul Carey's wife Patti. I didn't even realize the extent of her illness until after the Series had started. Even Paul himself didn't know about it until the eve of the Series. He had some suspicions, but really didn't know until we began our broadcast.

To me, the gutsiest performance of the World Series didn't happen on the diamond. It happened in our radio booth. It was the performance of Paul Carey who worked under tension and pressure which would have been unbearable for a lesser man.

He broadcast most of the series knowing that his wife Patti had been stricken with a malignant brain tumor.

First inklings of impending tragedy came on the Sunday the Tigers left for San Diego. We were gathering at Tiger Stadium, ready to board the bus for the airport.

"Isn't Patti going on the trip with us?" I asked Paul.

"No," he answered. "She's not feeling well. She's having dizzy spells, terrible headaches, and a loss of memory. She'll have to stay here and undergo tests."

The next day in San Diego, Paul was very concerned. He had talked with several friends about the situation. To them, some of Patti's symptoms seemed ominous.

"I'm worried," he said. "She just hasn't been like herself lately. I fear the worst."

Nevertheless, he went about his tasks. Remember that Paul serves not only as announcer of the Tiger games; he is also the producer and the engineer. Most stations have an engineer who travels with the announcers and handles all the technical problems. Many have producers who are in charge of spotting the commercials, keeping scores up-to-date and cueing the announcers. Paul is the only big league announcer who has to double-up with these chores. So, there is an extra burden on him.

Yet, he went about his duties in a professional way. We picked up our credentials. Sports director Frank Beckmann, Paul and I attended the Tiger workout at San Diego's Jack Murphy Stadium, checked out the booth, and readied ourselves for the broadcast the next day of the first World Series game.

Patti's tests were underway back in Detroit. Paul still had no word on the results.

My heart went out to him in this situation. I knew how close the two were. Married 23 years, they had no children. For years they had lived in a Royal Oak apartment but, just recently, they had bought their first home.

"I'm a homeowner now," Paul told me. "I didn't realize what it meant before. Finally, we have a place of our own."

They had spent a lot of time and money . . . new drapes, new rugs, many renovations. During the summer, Paul put a deck on the house for Patti. "Now, she can sit out and enjoy the sun while I'm away at work," he said.

They were looking forward to the fall when they'd be together with some time off for Paul . . . times when they could just be with each other.

Now this specter of Patti's illness was dominating Paul's whole existence.

Still, there was a job to be done. And he did it. It was his first World Series broadcast—something he'd dreamed of since boyhood. The team he had loved since his Mt. Pleasant boyhood was competing in the World Series with him at the microphone.

There were added duties. More time sold before and after the game. More programming. Highlights to be re-recorded and played back. The post-game interview with Alan Trammell, and, of course, the added pressure of broadcasting the biggest sports event in Detroit history.

And still not knowing Patti's condition.

He didn't hear any definite news until the Tigers returned to Detroit for the third game.

"How's Patti?" I asked him in the booth before the third game.

"It's not good," he said. "Two different doctors have told me they think she has a malignant brain tumor. There'll be more tests, but it doesn't look good."

"What about San Diego? If we have to go back there, can you make the trip?" I asked.

"No, I'll stay here," he said. "I was working when my Dad died, and I was working when my mother died. I'll be damned if I'm working when Patti dies."

Tears filled his eyes. His voice broke. That great voice—the voice which had been likened to the voice of God—couldn't get out the words.

I tried to comfort him. I tried so hard . . .

The broadcast went on. He did his job so well, nobody could guess how much he was suffering.

The next day he had more definite news.

Patti would have to undergo a brain operation. The surgeons would take tissue from her brain and do a biopsy. The doctors were sure they would find a malignancy.

Paul continued to broadcast.

Here he was in the midst of the happiest time for the Tigers. They had swept through the season and the play-offs and now they were winning the World Series.

But for Paul, it was the saddest time of his life.

Finally the Tigers won. Paul went to the clubhouse. His heart was heavy, but he became a part of the jubilation of the championship clubhouse. Wet with champagne, he shouted congratulations to the players and elicited their happy yells and comments.

I raced to the clubhouse to join him and Frank Beckmann. I went into Sparky Anderson's office and brought him over to Paul and the mike. The two of us talked with Sparky. He answered our questions and then closed his comments by turning to Paul and saying:

"And Paul, all our blessings at this time go to you and Patti."

Sparky (and my wife Lulu) were the only two I had told about Paul and Patti.

But Sparky, even in that climactic time of his team's triumph, had the compassion to remember what Paul was going through. His pain and suffering continued into the winter—and even beyond. Before the 1985 baseball season started, Patti had died.

So, to me the best, the gutsiest performance of the 1984 World Series was that of my partner Paul Carey.

3

They Also Serve, Who Only Sign The Checks

THEY CAN'T PITCH, OR HIT OR RUN, BUT SOMETIMES they get as much ink in the newspapers and magazines or as much time on radio and TV as the Dave Winfields, the Mike Schmidts, or the Tom Lasordas.

They are the men who furnish the money or the entrepreneurship—or both. They are the owners.

The old-time baseball writers called them moguls, or magnates, or nabobs. The modern writers have dubbed them ''The Lords of Baseball.'' But, they are the brains behind a team. They are the persons who build the organizations.

I've known many of them in my career. I've worked for a handful. They're as different as the players they hire or the media types they tolerate.

My first was Earl Mann in Atlanta. Earl didn't actually own the Atlanta Cracker team in the Southern Association. He was the operating head of the organization. At that time—1934—the team was owned by the Coca-Cola company.

Mann had sold peanuts at old Ponce de Leon Park. He ushered at a local movie house. He entered baseball's officialdom as a worker in the Brooklyn farm system, finally coming to Atlanta to oversee the Cracker franchise.

The first full-length feature I ever wrote for *The Sporting News* was about Earl Mann. "From peanut vendor to Cracker president" was the way the headline read. I had been *The Sporting News* Atlanta correspondent for almost a year before I met him.

In 1934 *The Sporting News* had no correspondent for Atlanta. Noting that, I sat down and wrote the editor and applied for the job.

I was 16 years old and still in high school. I had never written anything at the time. However, I didn't mention that in my letter. Also, in an effort to make myself seem older and more mature, I signed my letter W. Ernest Harwell instead of Ernie Harwell.

My letter was answered by E. G. Brands, *The Sporting News* editor.

". . . If you care to take a crack at it, we would be glad to have you submit a few stories within the next month or so to give us an idea of your ability to cover the field. If satisfactory, we will be glad to make arrangements with you for acting as our representative in Atlanta. If this is satisfactory, will you shoot the stuff along?"

Brands's letter was dated August 7, 1934.

I did shoot some stuff along and in the August 16 issue of *The Sporting News* my first article appeared— "Saddened Crackers Tumble" was the headline.

I continued to write for *The Sporting News*, attending the games and re-writing local stories. At 16, I didn't have the courage to contact Mann or manager Spencer Abbott or any of the players.

"Who is this guy, W. Earnest Harwell?" Mann kept asking the media people around town. Nobody knew. Then finally, I showed up to write a feature about Earl.

He was most gracious to me. My boyhood fears had been needless. Through the years we became friends and he was always one of my staunchest supporters, both in my writing and broadcasting careers.

The owners and chief executives of those Southern league clubs were a lively bunch. They were always playing tricks and practical jokes on each other.

The most renowned was Joe Engel, nationally publicized as "The Barnum of the Bushes." A one-time pitcher and later a scout, Joe was the ebullient owner of the Chattanooga Lookouts. He once staged an exhibition game in which a girl pitcher named Jackie Mitchell fanned Babe Ruth and Lou Gehrig. He installed canaries in his park to sing for the customers. He was the first owner to sponsor a give-away at a game. One night he gave away a house and lot. He even traded his shortstop John Jones to the Charlotte team for a Thanksgiving turkey.

Mann was not as flamboyant as his pal Joe Engel. But he was a smart operator. He was one of the last—if not the last—of the independent operators of a baseball team in America. Finally, he had to succumb to join the Boston Braves farm system; but he held out longer than any of his colleagues.

Mann's system was simple. Build a scouting staff, sign young prospects, develop them, and sell them to the majors. Put a good team on the field and attract the fans. For more than 15 consecutive years, the Atlanta team drew over 300,000 paid admissions. And at that time, the population of the city was around 250,000. When Earl signed a prospect, he promised him part of the money if he sold that prospect to the majors.

Luke Appling and Bill Goodman, two American League batting champions, were among his stars. They signed with Earl, played with the Crackers, and went on to make their mark in the majors.

My first baseball play-by-play was for Earl Mann. After a short stint in '43 while I was in the Marines, I came back from overseas to work regularly for him in 1946. With Kiki Cuyler managing, that 1946 team won the pennant. Billy Goodman, Lloyd Gearhart, Bill Ayers, and Earl McGowan were some of the '46 Crackers who went on to the big leagues.

Gearhart figured in a little domestic episode which is still chuckled about in the Harwell household.

My first son, Bill, was three years old. His mother had told him, "Bill, the Lord is going to bring us a baby soon."

One afternoon Lloyd Gearhart rang our doorbell. Lulu was busy and I was in the backyard. Bill answered the ring. He came running to his mother.

"Mama, Mama," he shouted, "the Lord is here and he doesn't have our baby."

Broadcasting in the minors was tougher than in the majors. Nobody had the averages figured for you. There were no team brochures with biographical sketches of the players. The broadcaster dug up all his information on his own. I would visit each team at a downtown hotel during the day, interviewing each player. For stats, I would buy the out-of-town newspapers, scan the box scores, and bring my averages up-to-date.

After each broadcast, I'd ride home on the streetcar late at night and figure the averages on the way.

That first year I seldom broadcast a complete game at night. WATL was a Mutual outlet and the night games couldn't get on the air until 10 o'clock. If the game were over, I'd do a re-cap. Most nights I'd join the game in progress and broadcast the final two or three innings. Either way, I was paid the same—$25 per game.

On Sundays and holidays, I did a full game.

Also, I got all the Wheaties I could eat—and more. Each Cracker batter received a free case of Wheaties whenever he hit a home run. Most of the players were single, so they gave me their Wheaties. Not only did the Harwells enjoy the cereal but our dog, Bluegrass, also became a Wheaties lover.

It was a good time for me. I loved my job. I worked hard and dreamed of being a big league baseball announcer. On Saturday afternoons I did re-creations on WAGA of a major league game of the week. That same evening I would broadcast a Cracker game—either live or re-created over WATL.

My broadcasting in 1946 would lead to my association with another baseball executive. He was perhaps the most respected in baseball history—Branch Rickey.

Jim Murray once wrote: "Branch Rickey can appraise a baseball prospect from the window of a passing train."

Mr. Rickey didn't see me from a train, but he found out about me. And he came after me.

But before Rickey came into my life and career, there was another development.

After the 1946 season I signed a contract for the first time. Previously, I had worked without a contract. But Old Gold was satisfied with my work in '46 and was to be the full-time 1947 sponsor of the Cracker game broadcasts. So, in November of 1946 I signed a contract with them for the following season.

"What if I get a big league offer?" I asked.

"No problem," was the answer. "Big league offer, you can go. We wouldn't hold you to the contract."

In less than three weeks, the ad agency for Chesterfield contacted me. Could I come to New York and broadcast the New York Giants' games in 1947 with Frankie Frisch?

Wow! I was overwhelmed. I was—until I checked with Old Gold.

"No, we can't release you from the contract."

"Why not? You said you would."

"Yes, we did. But this is a different situation. We broadcast the Dodger games. Chesterfield is our number one rival. We couldn't possibly let you do the Giants games for them."

Earl Mann intervened. He pleaded with the Old Gold people. They remained adamant. Harwell can't go to the Giants. He must stay and do the Cracker games for us.

"There goes my dream," I told myself, "my chance at the big leagues. Another opportunity like that may never come again."

I was wrong.

In January 1948, I got a long-distance call from Brooklyn.

"Ernie Harwell?"

"Yes."

"I'm Arthur Mann, Mr. Branch Rickey's assistant at Brooklyn. I'd like to come to Atlanta tomorrow and talk with you."

I gasped and managed to hold on to the phone.

The next afternoon Arthur Mann was in my living room, discussing the possibility of my broadcasting for the Dodgers.

"Ernie," he told me, "Mr. Rickey knows all about you. He has had several of his trusted people hear your broadcasting. He has checked out your background, your education, your habits, and your family life. He is very much interested in you."

The plan was for me to broadcast the Dodger games in July when Red Barber would take leave to do the Olympics in England for CBS. I would work with Connie Desmond. No problem about a release from Atlanta since Old Gold sponsored baseball in both cities.

"Also, Mr. Rickey has another plan," Arthur Mann told me. "He may want you to broadcast the road games the second half of the season. Red Barber may not want to travel with the team. If so, we'd like to have you ready to travel and broadcast our games. We'll be in touch."

I was in Gainesville, Florida, covering the Crackers' spring training when Arthur Mann got in touch.

"Not a word to anybody about this, Ernie, but Mr. Rickey will meet you Tuesday at 5 p.m. at the Battle House in Mobile," Mann told me. Then he immediately hung up.

I hopped a plane Tuesday morning. I arrived at the Battle House in mid-afternoon and waited. No Mr.

Rickey. No anybody. I ate dinner in my room, waiting by the phone. No call. No messages.

Finally, I phoned Arthur Mann at his home in Brooklyn.

"Mr. Rickey had to change his plans," he said. "Don't worry. You'll hear from us."

Slightly bewildered, I flew back to training camp in Gainesville. Two weeks later I was back in Atlanta. A letter came from Arthur Mann. Once again, he mapped out the Rickey scheme, telling me to plan to be in Brooklyn at least part of the summer. Mr. Rickey would be in touch.

Hadn't I heard that before?

In five days I received a phone call. It was Rache Bell, who had coached my American Legion sandlot team. He was a scout for the Dodgers and a Rickey favorite.

"Ernie," he said. "This is important. A certain person wants to see you at the Ansley Hotel tomorrow morning at 8 o'clock. Be in the coffee shop."

I was in the coffee shop at 8. So was Branch Rickey.

"I have little time," he told me, "but I must talk with you about broadcasting for the Dodgers."

Then this wonderful man, who didn't have much time, took an hour-and-a-half with me. He revealed his future plans for me. Essentially, the plan was the same as Arthur Mann had outlined for me earlier.

"Keep the faith," he said as he left. "We'll be in touch."

The Cracker season opened and I was broadcasting again in the Southern League. But my ear was cocked for a word or two from Brooklyn. I'd missed my New

York Giant opportunity, but maybe the Dodger chance would be realized.

Nothing happened.

I worked into mid-season.

The Olympics were about to start. Barber would have to leave. Still, I'd heard nothing.

Then in late July I read an item in the paper. Barber had been felled by a bleeding ulcer in Pittsburgh and rushed to the hospital—he was in critical condition.

That afternoon Arthur Mann called.

"Mr. Rickey wants you to come to Brooklyn right away. Red is seriously ill. We didn't call about the Olympics because we had arranged for celebrity announcers to appear with Connie. But now we need you."

I flew to Brooklyn. I went to Ebbets Field and saw several innings with Branch Rickey in his box. We agreed that I would return in several days and start broadcasting the Dodger games with Connie Desmond.

But before I left Atlanta, there had to be a trade.

Rickey wanted me. Earl Mann, my boss, said all right. But he demanded that Rickey send the Crackers a catcher named Cliff Dapper, who at that time was on their farm club in Montreal. I went to Brooklyn and Dapper came to the Crackers for the 1949 season and also became the Atlanta manager.

When I went to Brooklyn to broadcast, I forgot to pack a tie. My next meeting with Mr. Rickey was at 8:30 a.m. at the Dodger office on Montague Street. I got up, dressed, and then realized I needed a tie. (These days such an oversight doesn't seem important, but in those days it loomed large.)

I headed out of the Bossert hotel toward the office.

On the way I saw several clothing stores, all closed. Finally, I spotted a clerk in one of them. That store too was closed. I knocked on the glass and the clerk came to the door. I explained my problem. He let me in, sold me a tie, and I was on my way.

Rickey welcomed me and lit a cigar.

I asked if he would put into a contract our earlier agreement.

"Why, Ernie," he said, "I don't understand. Branch, Jr., has worked for me for years without a contract."

"Yes, Mr. Rickey," I said. "But Branch, Jr., is a member of your own family. Besides, something might happen to either one of us and if there is nothing in writing, there could be misunderstandings."

"I see. I understand," he said. "It'll all be put into a letter."

I returned to the Bossert hotel. My first game was scheduled that night at Ebbets Field. All I could do was wait. I knew no one in Brooklyn. I had never seen a National League game. In fact, the only regular season major league game I had seen was at Comiskey Park in Chicago in 1934. I didn't even know where Ebbets Field was or how to get there.

So, I went back to the hotel room and waited.

The game that night was rained out.

My nervousness increased. The walls of my room were moving in on me.

Finally, the skies cleared and I caught the subway to Ebbets Field. Connie Desmond introduced me around and everybody was friendly. As I was standing by the Brooklyn batting cage during practice, I heard a shout: "Hey, Ernie."

It was Russ Meyer, the Chicago Cub pitcher. He'd

been at Nashville when I was broadcasting the Atlanta games. Meyer's greeting made me feel warm inside. I realized that here in this strange park, in this strange city, trying to do a strange job, I had met a friend. Russ pitched that night against the Dodgers. But he left early. He was ejected from the game for his protest of a safe call on Jackie Robinson's steal of home in the first inning.

I don't remember much else about that first broadcast. I was too excited. I got through it and took a streetcar back to the Bossert.

I was now a big league announcer.

I continued to announce until the end of the season. Then Rickey hired me to replace Ted Husing as his announcer for the Brooklyn Dodger football team in the All-America Conference. He didn't ask if I'd ever broadcast football or any other details. He simply hired me.

Red Barber's health improved and he returned to duty in mid-September. He, Connie Desmond, and I completed the season. Red was still weak and didn't work much.

Rickey took an option on my services for the next season and I looked forward to my first full year as a Dodger announcer. Red, Connie, and I would be sharing the radio and TV coverage.

The Giants called. They wanted me for the next season. I told them no. I was just getting settled in and didn't want to move that quickly. But it was good to be wanted.

I stayed on with the Dodgers for the 1949 season. Brooklyn was a great place to work. Ebbets Field was a gem of a ball park and the legendary fans were loyal, demonstrative, and very knowledgeable.

The Dodgers were my first big league team and will always have a special place in my heart. Such great guys, too—Jackie Robinson, Pee Wee Reese, Gil Hodges, Carl Erskine, and Rex Barney.

They won the pennant in Philadelphia on the final day of the season. Contrasted to the wild celebrations of recent years, 1949's climax was mild. In fact, for the players there was no celebration. I remember riding back to New York on the train. There were eight or ten players in the club car, along with some of the media. One of the photographers came in.

"Hey, here are some Dodger pennants," he told the players. "Wave the pennants for my picture."

After the World Series, the Giants came after me again. This time I succumbed. I hated to leave Brooklyn, but the offer was better. Besides, I would be working with only one announcer, Russ Hodges, instead of two.

There was one hitch. The Dodgers had an option on my services for the next year. Branch Rickey was in the Mayo Clinic in Rochester, Minnesota for a checkup, so I called Branch, Jr.

"We'd like to keep you," Branch, Jr. told me. "But it sounds like a good offer. I'm sure Dad wouldn't want to stand in your way. Let me contact him for you."

Several days later I received a handwritten letter from Branch, Sr. He gave me his blessing to leave.

For the next four seasons I broadcast for the Giants. Russ Hodges and I shared radio and television, with Chesterfield the sole sponsor for all the broadcasts. I had traded bosses, too—Branch Rickey for Horace Stoneham.

What a difference between those two!

Rickey was a Bible-reading teetotaler. Stoneham was a heavy drinker who loved to party. Rickey was actively involved in most every phase of running his club. Stoneham usually couldn't be bothered with details. Rickey had played, coached, and managed; Stoneham was the son of a wealthy owner, Rickey had scrimped, struggled, and saved to own a piece of the action; Stoneham had inherited his share.

Earl Mann once told me that in the late Forties he wanted Mel Ott to manage the Atlanta Crackers. Ott had retired as Giant manager and was working with the farm system.

"I tried to get in touch with Stoneham to discuss a deal," Earl said. "But I couldn't locate him. Nobody else in the Giants' organization had the authority to make the deal, so I was never able to hire Ott as my manager."

In 1950, the Giants brought up a rookie first baseman, Harold Joseph (Tookie) Gilbert, from Nashville. We were in Pittsburgh at the time, staying at the old Schenley hotel. Stoneham decided to combine the announcement of the move with a dinner party for the writers and announcers.

We all gathered in his room and he told us the news. Then we settled down for drinks and steak dinners. After dinner, most of us drifted away. But—as always with Horace—there were a few left. When this happened, Horace would insist that no others leave. Two or three would have to stay—or else. After all, he was the boss.

"Sit-sy, sit-sy," Horace would mumble. The drinks

had thickened his tongue, but the regulars still could understand. They sat and sat and sat. As the night wore on, the small and sturdy band became hungry.

"Room service, call room service," muttered Stoneham.

Soon the room service waiter appeared with another round of steaks. Nobody knew it at the time, but the waiter was also the elevator operator in those lonely morning hours.

"Waiter," Horace told him. "Sit-sy. Sit-sy. You gotta stay here with us and talk baseball. Sit-sy."

The waiter protested.

"Mr. Stoneham. I got my job to do. I've got to get back to the elevator."

"No, son. Sit-sy. Stay with us."

Stoneham got out of his chair and locked the door.

"Now, you'll stay," he told the waiter.

He did stay. He stayed all night. The patrons of the Schenley hotel who came down to breakfast had no elevator to ride. They had to find another way to get to their morning meal. But Stoneham had his audience.

When Stoneham was partying—and it could happen any time of day or night—he had to have company. Usually, he wanted his manager. When I was with the Giants, the manager was Leo Durocher. He didn't want to party with Horace.

When he got a call from Horace (or Eddie Brannick, the traveling secretary, calling for Horace), Leo would say: "I'll be right there." But seldom did he come.

When sober, Stoneham was a true gentleman. He was gracious with the ladies. He was a loyal friend. Also, he was a sharp and knowledgeable baseball man.

In December 1949, Stoneham pulled off a deal which

brought the Giants from nowhere in the standings to two pennants in four years.

The '49 Giants, under Leo Durocher, had finished fifth, 24 games behind the pennant-winning Dodgers. Stoneham began to look around for Durocher-type players.

At the winter meetings in December, he had his deal. From the Boston Braves he obtained the two men he and Leo wanted—Eddie Stanky and Alvin Dark. Horace and Braves' GM John Quinn had a difficult time completing the transaction because Boston insisted on getting the Giant outfielder Bobby Thomson. Stoneham refused to part with Thomson who had power and also running speed. Finally the Braves agreed to take Willard Marshall instead. The trade was finalized at the winter meetings. The Giants got Stanky and Dark and sent the Braves Marshall, Buddy Kerr, Sid Gordon, and Sam Webb.

Horace was rapped by some of the writers for the deal. He was praised by others.

One wrote: "Neither team won the pennant with this deal."

He was wrong. The Giants won the pennant in 1951 and again in 1954 because of that very transaction.

I had departed the Giants in 1954 when they won the World Championship, but I was there when they pulled off the famous Miracle of Coogan's Bluff in 1951. It was the most thrilling season of my broadcasting career.

Stanky and Dark were the heart of that team. The brash, frank Stanky and the shy, deeply religious and courteous Dark were a great combination. Inseparable both on and off the field, each was a dedicated competitor. Each loved to win and hated to lose.

The Giants' rush to the pennant is an oft-told tale. They were 13½ games back of the Dodgers in mid-August, caught them the final weekend and they beat them in the final game of the three-game playoff.

On August 9 at Ebbets Field the Dodgers beat the Giants for the twelfth time in 15 meetings. They were on a roll. The Giants could do nothing but sit and listen as the Dodgers celebrated in their clubhouse across the way.

Taunts from the Dodgers cut through the thin partition into a silent Giant clubhouse.

"Leo, Leo, you in there? Eat your heart out, Leo. Yeah, that's your team, Leo. Nobody else wants it."

The Dodgers were singing, "Roll Out the Barrel, we've got the Giants on the run."

The Giants could detect the high-pitched voice of Jackie Robinson through the thin door. Then they heard him pounding his bat against the partition.

"Stick that bat down your throat, you black nigger son of a bitch," Stanky yelled.

Next to Eddie was Monte Irvin, himself a graduate from the ranks of Negro baseball. But now Monte's loyalties were with the Giants.

"That goes for me too," he shouted toward Robinson.

Did those verbal fireworks provide a spark for the Giant comeback? Who knows?

Anyway, Leo's team began to make its move. They swept a doubleheader with Brooklyn and eventually won 16 in a row. In less than three weeks, they cut the Dodger lead to five games. They kept coming on until the end of the season. Brooklyn didn't fold. The Dodgers won 24 of their last 44 games. But, the Giants won 37 of their last 44.

The Giants were to finish the season with two games in Boston. They were off Friday night, September 28. The Dodgers lost in Philadelphia that night and the race was tied. Each team won its next two games, forcing a three-game playoff.

The Giants' victory over Boston had come earlier that Sunday afternoon. So, we had to wait on the Dodger-Philly result. I remember listening to the radio in the Giant clubhouse. When we left for the train station the Phils were leading. We finally got the word in Providence. Chub Feeney, the Giants' VP then, re-boarded the train.

"Dodgers won," he said "Robinson hit a homer in the fourteenth to win it, 9–8. Show up at Ebbets Field tomorrow for the first playoff game."

This was the first sport series ever telecast coast-to-coast. Before then, any telecast in New York was seen two days later on the West Coat. Now, because of the co-axial cable, the Dodger-Giant series would be viewed as it happened. CBS-TV picked up the Dodger broadcast of that first game and sent it across the nation.

Jim Hearn pitched the biggest game of his career and the Giants won the first game, 3–1. Bobby Thomson's two-run homer was the vital blow.

The two teams moved to the Polo Grounds. It was the Giants' broadcasters' turn to go coast-to-coast. NBC-TV picked up our telecast. Russ Hodges worked the first and last three innings and I telecast the middle three. We had a rain delay of about 50 minutes during my portion of the telecast. I remember filling all the time myself. Our booth was so cramped it was impossible to get anybody else to the mike for an interview.

We had a great shot of Yankee Stadium, across the river. The Yanks had won the American League pennant and would host the winner of the National League playoffs in the first World Series game.

"So near and yet so far, for these two teams here today at the Polo Grounds," I said. "But one of them will be there."

The Dodgers won that second game, 10–0, behind Clem Labine, a young right-hander who had spent most of the season in the bullpen. That set the stage for the big one.

These two teams had played 156 games each and they were still tied. One more and it would all be over.

I had a feeling at the time that both teams were weary and that everybody was pushing to get through that final meeting.

As I drove to the Polo Grounds from my Larchmont home, I told myself how lucky I was to be in on this one. I would be on NBC-TV coast-to-coast on the biggest game in baseball history. Hodges, my partner, would have to settle for radio. I would be the only TV announcer, but there were at least four other radio broadcasts: the Dodger network, Liberty, Mutual, and KMOX of St. Louis.

When Russ and I were eating lunch, he said: "Ernie, I think it's my time today on TV."

"No," I said. "Remember, you were on yesterday. I did the middle three of that game on TV. I've got the first and last three on TV today."

"Oh," he said. "I guess you're right."

So, I was on NBC-TV coast-to-coast when Bob Thomson hit his famous home run in the ninth to win the game for the Giants, 5–4.

Over the years people have asked me: "Ernie, what did you say when Thomson hit his home run?"

"It's gone," I tell them. As soon as Bobby hit the ball I said, "It's gone." Then I let the picture tell the story. Right after I had said those two words I had quick misgivings. Andy Pafko had backed up against the left-field wall and was waiting. "Oh," I told myself, "suppose Andy catches it!" But the ball sailed into the seats and history was made.

The next two years weren't good ones for the Giants and Horace Stoneham. In the spring of 1952, Monte Irvin broke his ankle in Denver and nothing seemed to go right after that. Willie Mays was drafted by the Army and the Giants finished second to their hated rivals, the Dodgers. The bottom fell out in '53. Poor pitching and all-around mediocrity led to a fifth-place finish.

In December, I found out the Giants weren't renewing my option for the following year. As in most firings, the man getting fired was the last to find out. No reasons were given, but I was not returning.

When I was fired, my newspaper friends in New York were very supportive. Harold Rosenthal, one of my closest friends, was most encouraging. Roger Kahn took the Giants to task in a long article about me in the *Herald-Tribune*.

"Ernie, you don't really grow up until you've been fired at least once," Bill Corum, the *Journal American* columnist, told me.

Others who wrote in support of Ernie Harwell were Dick Young of the *Daily News*, Arch Murray of the

Post, Max Kase of the *Journal American*, Art Richman of the *Mirror* and Milt Richman of the *United Press*.

They were kind enough to say that I'd have no trouble locating another job. And they were correct. Right away, Baltimore beckoned. The city was returning to big league baseball and within a month after I heard the Giants' bad news, I received good news from the Orioles. I was going to Baltimore to be number one announcer for the new American League entry.

It was there I met a baseball executive I came to admire. He was Jack Dunn, III. Jack was a powerful, behind-the-scenes factor in Baltimore baseball but never really received the credit he deserved.

"Dunnie" was responsible for the smooth transition of baseball in Baltimore from the minor league Orioles to the major league Orioles. Jack was president and general manager of the minor league franchise.

When the new owners took over and the Orioles became major league, Jack stayed on as a traveling secretary. Later he became assistant general manager and now is vice president, stadium operations and a member of the board of directors.

For more than 75 years the name of Dunn has symbolized baseball in Baltimore. It started in 1905 with the first Jack Dunn, Jack's grandfather. He joined the Baltimore team when they were in the Eastern League. The original Dunn played second base and managed the team in 1906. Three years later he bought the club from Ned Hanlon. Dunn had no backers. He purchased the club with his lifetime savings, $70,000, and continued as president and manager until his death.

Jack Dunn's Orioles won seven straight International League pennants. More importantly, he developed and sold to the majors many great stars. Babe Ruth was a Dunn discovery. Jack found the Babe at St. Mary's Industrial school in Baltimore when his uncontrolled nature had been somewhat harnessed by a firm Brother Matthias.

"That's Dunnie's Babe," the hard-bitten Oriole veterans said when the 19-year-old youngster reported to camp. In less than a year the Babe was pitching with the Boston Red Sox and then went on to the Yankees to become baseball's most colorful slugger.

Dunn also developed and sold to the big leagues Lefty Grove, Ernie Shore, George Earnshaw, and Max Bishop. Dunn spurned offers to join a big league club as an executive. He wanted to pass his club along to his only son, Jack, Jr. Jack, Jr.—the present Jack's dad— had begun to work side-by-side with his famous father. A great future lay ahead of him. Then, as the Orioles completed their 1922 spring training, Jack Dunn, Jr. died of pneumonia.

It was a tragic blow to the father. He gave up managing and with heavy heart confined his work to the front office. He put the uniform on again as a manager in 1928, but died in October of that year.

Jack, Jr.'s widow, Mary Dunn, took over the team, turning down numerous prospective buyers. When she died in 1943, she willed the club to Jack III with the stipulation he become absolute owner on his thirtieth birthday.

Before Jack had officially taken over, he was well-grounded in baseball. His apprenticeship began when he attended the games with his mother. While in high school he became traveling secretary of the Orioles at the age of 16. In 1946 Jack gave an early display of his now renowned versatility. He served as president and general manager of the Oriole farm club at Centreville in the Eastern Shore League. He also caught and played first base.

He came back to Baltimore as traveling secretary in 1947 and 1948. He took over the club presidency in the winter of '48. When Tommy Thomas resigned as manager in mid-season of 1949, Jack again became a manager. The next year he decided to concentrate on the front office. He hired Nick Cullop as his field manager and remained president and general manager of the club until he sold the franchise to the American League Orioles.

During the transition period Jack was especially helpful. His steady hand and Baltimore's great respect for him helped the Oriole organization over rough spots. The new management made mistakes in the early going, but Dunnie was there to smooth the pathway.

Edward Bennett Williams, the owner, and GM Hank Peters are fortunate to have a man like Jack Dunn still working in their front office and lending his expertise in so many phases of the business to their organization.

About mid-way in my Oriole broadcasting stint, George Kell was traded by the White Sox to Baltimore. In 1956 George was beaned and during his recovery period, sat in the radio-TV booth.

"Now, you're learning the art of free-loading," I kidded him. "All the hot dogs you can eat and all the pop you can drink."

After a couple of games, I asked him to broadcast an inning for us. He did. He liked it and the listening audience liked him. George retired as a player and then returned to the game through TV and radio—first with a pre-game show on CBS-TV in 1958 and then working the following season with Van Patrick on the Tiger broadcasts.

In 1959 the Orioles finished their season with a three-game series in Yankee stadium. After the Friday night game I was back in my room at the Roosevelt hotel when the phone rang. It was George Kell.

"Ernie, Mr. Harry Sisson, the Tiger vice-president asked me to call you," he said. "Van Patrick won't be back as Tiger announcer next year. I recommended you to replace him. Would you like to work with me on the Tiger games?"

The call surprised me. I thought Patrick was in solid.

"Are you sure about Van?" I asked. "I wouldn't want to be pushing him out."

"No doubt about it," George said. "If you don't replace him, somebody else will."

"Well, I like Baltimore. And I can stay there," I said. "But Detroit's always been a favorite spot for me. Tell Mr. Sisson I'd be glad to consider the job."

During the '59 World Series, I flew to Detroit and signed on with the Tigers.

Harry Sisson was the man who made the deal with me, but I'd be working for several owners. The Tigers were owned by a syndicate which had purchased the franchise from the Briggs family in the mid-Fifties.

About the same time I became a Tiger announcer, the syndicate hired veteran baseball official Bill DeWitt as the club's president. Bill and his brother Charlie had started in St. Louis. They had nursed the old St. Louis Browns through years of financial struggle. Bill had worked for other clubs over the years and came to the Detroit organization from the Commissioner's office.

From his early scrimp-and-save days with the Browns, DeWitt had become a cut-the-corners efficiency expert. He was taking over the presidency of a company with an almost country club atmosphere—a real contrast to the environment in which DeWitt was used to working. DeWitt jumped in with both feet.

"Too much time wasted by the telephone switchboard operators," he pointed out. He visited the trainer's room to check on trainer Jack Hommel. "How many vitamins are you buying a year?" he asked. "Why are you paying so much for them?"

DeWitt touched the nerve of every department. Each day he made his rounds, carrying 3×5 index cards in his pocket. He would pull out a card and admonish a different employee with each passing day.

He wasn't winning any popularity contests. Soon Tiger Stadium was abuzz with talk behind the boss's back.

"It's not the way we're used to doing it."

"What is he trying to do?"

"Who does he think he is?"

Those were some of the milder and more printable comments about the new president.

DeWitt's quest for economy even invaded his private existence and eventually led to his demise with the Detroit organization.

On our pre-game TV interview show, George Kell and I always awarded our guests with two gifts—a pair of Foot Joy shoes and a radio.

Early in 1960 we interviewed DeWitt. At the end of the show I announced on the air that Bill was receiving the two gifts. When the show was over, he came to me.

"Ernie," he said. "I know you give away shoes and a radio, but do you think I could have the cash instead?"

Meanwhile word about DeWitt and his actions kept drifting back to the ownership. Late in the summer he took one more step which proved to be fatal.

Bill had settled into a large, old home in Grosse Pointe. It was so large and so old that it needed many repairs. DeWitt enlisted Jess Walls, stadium superintendent, Tony Kochivar, head groundskeeper, and all their charges, to work on his house.

On they came with spade and shovel, with hammer and saw, and a lot of muscles. They worked for several days, their curses ringing out over the sounds of hammer and saw. They were working for the man they called "Ole Bubble Eyes" (because some felt that he looked like a fat frog within a business suit), but unbeknownst to him, they were also working against him. They were delivering the final blow to his short-lived Tiger career.

The news soon reached the syndicate about the DeWitt renovation. His detractors in that group moved quickly. Soon he was out. John E. Fetzer, one of the members of the syndicate, took financial control of the franchise and became its president.

DeWitt did leave the Tigers a legacy. In his short term he made two bold trades—both with Frank Lane, the Cleveland Indians' GM. At the end of spring training, DeWitt swapped the Tiger batting champion Harvey Kuenn for the Indians' home run champion Rocky Colavito. It was the kind of swap I like to see. We get too few of that type. Most baseball trades involve nonentities—players who will help neither team. This one was a swap of two outstanding stars. The deal was worth a ton of newspaper ink for months.

The other transaction was even bolder. DeWitt and Lane swapped managers. With less than two months remaining in the 1960 season, Tiger manager Jimmy Dykes went to Cleveland and the Indians' manager Joe Gordon migrated to Detroit. Another transaction of great interest. I thought that both managers disliked the swap. They wouldn't say so publicly, but off-the-record each felt it was demeaning.

Dykes managed one more year—at Cleveland. Gordon managed in 1961 at Kansas City. Then in 1969, he returned to manage Kansas City again. After that he was through with baseball.

The beginning and the end of the Dykes-Gordon story added contrasting footnotes to Detroit sports journalism history. One provided a scoop for Joe Falls; the other went unnoticed.

On the eve of the swap, the Tigers were in New York. Falls got a telephone tip from Mo Siegel, Washington newspaperman, that the Tigers and the Indians would swap managers.

"I just had a drink with Nate Dolan of the Indians," Mo told Falls. "He guarantees it's going to happen."

Falls already had sensed that Dykes was out. But he had filed a story with his paper, *The Detroit Times*, that Billy Hitchcock would take over as interim manager.

He immediately called his office, killed the first story, and wrote his exclusive.

When Gordon quit the Tigers at the end of the season, the Detroit papers missed the story. Gordon did not like DeWitt. He decided to quit on the final day of the 1960 season. The Tigers were finishing out the schedule in Kansas City. They were in sixth place, 26 games behind the pennant-winning Yankees. There were no writers on the plane as we flew back to Detroit.

"I'm quitting," Joe told his players and all of the rest of us on the plane. He quit, but there was no one to write it.

In less than two months Gordon's nemesis, Bill DeWitt, was gone too.

Thus began the John E. Fetzer era in Tiger history.

Fetzer was good for the Tigers. The previous five years had proved that rule-by-committee didn't work. He took over with a strong hand and the move had a settling effect. Under Fetzer, Jim Campbell moved into a stronger position, becoming the Tigers' general manager at the end of the 1962 season.

From his radio-television empire, Fetzer brought a solid business acumen into baseball. He soon earned the respect of his fellow owners with his new concepts about the relationship between TV and baseball. He shaped the TV-baseball contracts which had been so beneficial to the game.

Fetzer delegated great authority in the Tiger operation to Jim Campbell. His confidence has been rewarded. Campbell has been a career man. He eats and sleeps baseball. To the media, he is one of the most trusted of all sports executives. His honesty and integrity have never been questioned.

Both Fetzer and Campbell have been good bosses for me. We've had very few differences. During the much-publicized Jose Feliciano National Anthem incident, Fetzer wrote me a letter, chastising me mildly for my participation in the event.

Campbell called me on the carpet because of a strange episode during the 1973 season. He was disturbed that

I had mistakenly announced over the air that a Tiger-California game had been postponed.

"Many fans left the park when you made that announcement," he told me. "Now they want their money back. What's the story?"

It was a rainy Friday night in Detroit. The game between the Tigers and California Angels was delayed. During a two-hour wait the phone in our radio booth rang. The call was from Hal Middlesworth, the Tiger PR director in the press box.

"Looks like the game will be called. If we call it, there'll be a doubleheader tomorrow. But don't announce it until you hear it on the intercom."

Thirty minutes later my partner Ray Lane, our engineer Howard Stitzel, and I heard this announcement over the intercom: "Game called. There'll be a doubleheader tomorrow."

"Turn the mike on, Stitz," I said. "I'll make the announcement on the air."

I made the announcement. I left the booth and Lulu and I began our drive home.

As we left Tiger Stadium, I noticed that many of the fans were leaving. But a number were staying around.

"Maybe they're afraid of getting wet," I thought. "Otherwise they'd be on their way."

As we were driving, I turned on Ray Lane's postgame show. He was giving scores. Suddenly, he stopped in the middle of a score.

"Wait a minute folks," he said. "We've just got word the game has not been postponed. It's still on. Ernie. Ernie, come on back wherever you are."

We turned around and headed toward Tiger Stadium. I went to the booth. Rain was still falling. In about 15 minutes, play began. With an eighth-inning rally the Tigers beat the Angels, 4–3, in the game that I declared was postponed.

That was the way I explained it to Campbell.

"But how did you get that first announcement from the press box?" he wanted to know.

"It came over the press box intercom," I said. "Lane and Stitzel and I—all three heard it."

Middlesworth, who was in the meeting, was adamant that no such announcement was ever made.

"Then, how could we have heard it?" I asked.

Campbell sided with Middlesworth. He couldn't believe we had heard the announcement.

The Tigers had to refund ticket money to the fans who had left early because of my on-the-air announcement. That didn't make Campbell very happy either.

Finally the meeting broke up with a "Don't let it happen again" admonition from Jim Campbell.

There were two possible explanations:

(1) Some jokester sneaked to the mike (without Middlesworth's knowledge) and made the announcement;

(2) Somebody made the announcement, saying "*If* the game is called, there'll be a doubleheader tomorrow." And somehow his finger might have been on the button and erased the first word—"if."

Once the incident was over it was over, as Yogi Berra might have put it.

That's one of the many qualities I admire in Jim Campbell. He can lay it on the line, but he doesn't hold a grudge. Also, you can always go in and talk with Jim. He can be stubborn and he can disagree with you, but he will always listen to you.

* * *

A new owner took over the Tigers in December 1983. Tom Monaghan, who made millions with his Domino Pizza chain, bought the club from John Fetzer for $51 million.

Monaghan is a modest, self-effacing man. He is an upstanding family man of great moral fiber. From his youth he has loved the Tigers.

In his first year as Tiger owner, Monaghan hit the jackpot; his team raced in front with a 35–5 record. They went on to win the Eastern Division, sweep Kansas City in the American League playoffs, and win the World Series easily from the San Diego Padres.

"If you ever find this team out of first place," I kidded him, "you'll probably sell the club."

After pizza and baseball, Monaghan's chief interest is architecture. His lifetime hero is Frank Lloyd Wright.

In mid-season I saw a page one story in the *New York Times* that remnants of a Frank Lloyd Wright house would be auctioned that afternoon in New York. I brought the clipping to Tom and gave it to him just before the Tiger game started.

During my break from the radio booth in the fourth inning, I wandered over to Monaghan's booth.

"I'm glad you showed me that clipping," he said. "My real estate man is on the phone right this minute, buying that Frank Lloyd Wright house."

Monaghan moves quickly and he gets what he wants.

As an owner he admits that he is still learning on the job. He has excellent mentors in John Fetzer and Jim Campbell and an outstanding GM in Bill Lajoie.

The owners come and go. They are as varied in makeup as the teams they own. Some find their names splashed across the newspapers of the nation; others are less known. All of them have made their contributions to the game with their successes, their mistakes, their brains, their money, and their egos. And sometimes they are even more fascinating than the players.

4

Things Bound to Happen
in Baseball

DURING SPRING TRAINING . . .
Six players who were traded during the off-season will be quoted as saying their former teams didn't give them a fair chance.

A rookie umpire will work the bases in the first exhibition game and his name will be misspelled in every story.

The third-string catcher will write two weekly columns for his hometown paper, then decide he doesn't want to continue.

A pitcher who last year trained in Arizona will tell the press he likes training in Florida better because "it's easier to work up a good sweat." Another pitcher will say that he prefers Arizona because it's hotter and drier.

The local Chamber of Commerce will throw a barbecue for the big-leaguers and only three regulars will show.

Four players will tell the GM to "play me or trade me."

A Latin American star will be missing from camp. He will report two weeks later because of "visa trouble."

Three pitchers will observe that the ball is a lot livelier this spring.

Writers and announcers will gripe about how bad the free food is this year. But they'll devour it just the same.

The first base coach will tell a writer, "I don't know where we'll finish this year, but I guarantee we'll improve over last season."

Taking a short cut, the bus driver will get lost on the way to a new ball park.

Of the 2,678 men asking for autographs, 2,345 will say that they're asking for their grandson or nephew.

Two rookies will be hospitalized for severe sunburn.

A local belly-dancer will pose for a photo with the manager in front of the dugout.

Three strangers will show up in the press box, sit there through the entire game and nobody will know who they are or where they came from.

The record machine will break down during the playing of the National Anthem.

On a Big League Team Bus . . .

The driver will be fat.

Above the dashboard he will have a new league baseball to be autographed by the players.

The player who wandered aimlessly off first base and was picked off in last night's game will give the driver directions to the ball park.

Before the bus has gone three blocks, at least four players will yell for more air conditioning.

An elderly lady will board the bus at a stoplight and ask, "Is this the D-bus to Glen Cove?"

The team manager will sit at the front of the bus. And the loudest stereos will blast from the back.

Somebody will have news—or at least a rumor—of a brand-new big league trade.

The ugliest man on the team will shout out of his window at a fairly attractive young lady—and tell her how ugly she is.

At least one player will be working a crossword puzzle.

The worst-dressed passengers will be members of the media.

During a Baseball Rain Delay . . .

Everybody will desert the box seat area, but three kids with plastic over their heads will remain there throughout the rain.

The organist will play "Raindrops Keep Falling on My Head," "Singing in the Rain," and four other rain songs.

A banner in the center-field bleachers will become so soaked that all the lettering will run together.

A rookie utility infielder will hope for more rain, so he can attend a downtown movie.

Three young ladies will run to the box seat section and try to talk with some of the players in the home dugout. The players will ignore them, but the bat boy will make points.

Four or five players will stay in each dugout. At least one player in each dugout will be fondling a bat.

Two sportswriters will locate a well-endowed lady in the stands and train binoculars on her.

Another writer will re-visit the press room to devour two more ham and cheese sandwiches.

A youngster will dash from the stands onto the field and slide on the tarp.

At the height of the downpour, some loud-mouth fan will yell at nobody in particular, ''Play ball.''

At the Winter Baseball Meeting . . .

All but 38 of the 1,750 delegates will congratulate each other for leaving frigid December weather for the mild climate of the convention city.

No trades will be made during the first two days; but writers will speculate in detail on 23 rumored transactions.

The convention's first deal will not be a blockbuster. It won't even be a driveway buster. A fifth-place team will trade a utility man who hit .203 for a sore-armed pitcher who was 2 and 8.

The oldest big league coach will sit in the lobby until only the cleaning ladies are left. The next morning he'll be the first man in the coffee shop.

A local photographer will pose an arriving general manager being greeted by the hotel manager. It will be the only time during the convention any of the delegates will see the hotel manager.

The bell captain will decide that baseball people tip better than the WCTU convention, but not as well as the International Funeral Directors.

At least one sportswriter will combine his coverage of the convention with his honeymoon.

In announcing each deal, every GM will state that it's

a deal which will help both clubs . . . then both clubs will announce that because of their latest transaction their team has become a viable contender for next season.

An old-time player who lives in the convention city will call on his ex-teammates, but none of them will remember his name.

The wife of a big league owner will go on a sight-seeing tour, sponsored by the local chamber of commerce, and she will lose one earring.

Six deals will fall through because players don't want to live and play in the cities they were traded to.

The hotel newsstand will run out of copies of *The Sporting News* and the *New York Times*.

Three potted plants in the lobby will die from smoke inhalation and alcohol poisoning.

The final banquet of the convention will feature a big-name singer; but most of the executives will miss the star's performance because they'll be in the bar trying to make a last-minute deal for a left-handed pitcher.

At the Sports Banquet . . .

There won't be a parking space for the main speaker.

The dinner will start 45 minutes late.

Whoever gives the invocation will refer at least once to the "Game of Life."

The speaker who "needs no introduction" will get a flowery one, lasting fourteen minutes.

The speaker who says, "I'll be brief," will make the longest speech of the evening.

The banqueters will be served a balanced meal—meaning that they'll have a 50–50 chance to survive.

The menu will consist of rubber chicken or cardboard beef, bullet peas, watery potatoes, and brick ice cream.

The banquet chairman will offend three committee members by forgetting to introduce them.

One waiter will drop a tray of food.

The ladies who did the cooking will be called from the kitchen to take a bow. One of them will be too bashful to appear.

The sound system will squeal and sputter.

The oldest joke will get the biggest laugh.

Youngsters will disrupt the dinner by charging the speakers' table and getting autographs.

The Mayor will apologize for leaving early because of an important civic meeting (actually, his weekly poker game).

The press table will empty the quickest.

5

"When I Ope My Lips, Let No Dog Bark"

Shakespeare, *Merchant of Venice*
Act I, Scene 1

IN THE EARLY DAYS OF RADIO, TWO MEN WERE THE
dominant sports announcers—Graham McNamee and
Ted Husing. Each started in the early 1920s. McNamee
lasted only a short while. Husing worked until the
1950s.

I knew McNamee only from listening to his glowing
descriptions when I was a youngster. He had no real
knowledge of sports. He had come to radio as a meat
salesman with a fine singing voice and was a pioneer
in the business when each day brought a new assignment. Innovations were regular happenings.

The famed Ring Lardner sat next to McNamee during
the 1924 World Series. After one of the games, Ring
wrote: "The Washington Senators and the New York
Giants must have played a double-header this afternoon—the game I saw and the game Graham McNamee
announced."

Color and drama came first with McNamee. Facts didn't bother him one way or the other.

In those days the sports announcer was a professional voice who came from the studio to the game 30 minutes before the first pitch, bought a scorecard, and started talking. McNamee was typical of that genre.

Then along came Ted Husing, and the entire concept of sports announcing underwent a drastic change.

Husing was the first sports announcer who prepared for a game in a thorough, methodical way. He would talk to the players and coaches. He would attend practice sessions. He would study the strategy. He was always ready.

Ted also had an outstanding voice, resonant and smooth. He had a clear, yet dramatic style. He was supremely confident. And he sprinkled his broadcast with a sharp sense of humor. But, most of all, he prepared.

Red Smith put it this way:

"A great deal was said about the qualities that made him great . . . about his voice, his gift of gab, about how he could dramatize the event he was covering, about his flair for color. Everything they said was true, but nobody came flat out with the one big reason why he has never been touched.

"The reason he has been the best, it says here, is that he has been the most painstaking and accurate and knowledgeable reporter of facts covering sports on the air. Nobody ever worked harder at learning the game he was broadcasting."

The renowned Husing flair often got Ted in trouble. The most famous incident happened during a Harvard-

Dartmouth football game. Husing said: "Barry Wood (Harvard quarterback) is playing putrid football today compared to his performance of last week."

Telegrams of protest flooded CBS. Husing was banned from Harvard stadium. The press castigated him from coast-to-coast. The incident eventually proved fortunate for Ted. It projected him into the national spotlight. It humanized him to millions of sports fans. And (as he later admitted) it taught him a lesson in the choice of words.

Husing learned another lesson from Baseball Commissioner K. M. Landis. Baseball was never Ted's best announcing showcase, but he worked on several World Series. In fact, he broadcast his first Series some three weeks after landing his first radio job with WJZ in 1924. However, it was before the 1935 classic that the stoney-eyed Landis jumped down Husing's golden throat.

Ted had disagreed with the umpiring during the previous Series, expressing his disagreement in typically blunt Husing fashion. Landis told him that because of his criticism he would be restricted to a color assignment on the Series broadcast. Ted never again did any World Series play-by-play.

Yet, he remained a baseball fan. I still remember his kind comments about my broadcasting when I was working in New York for the Dodgers and the Giants.

However, if Husing did not respect the work of an announcer, he would rip him to pieces. I heard him unleash many a sarcastic tirade toward an announcer whose work he felt was shoddy or incompetent. Even in personal relationships Ted could be brutally outspoken. After a sports broadcasters' luncheon in New York, a young announcer stopped Ted and showed him some photos of his newborn baby.

"Cut it out," Husing told him. "I don't need to see any pictures of your baby. All babies look alike anyhow."

On the air, or off, Ted spoke his mind. And he hated mediocrity—in others and in himself. All of us in the broadcasting profession owe him a debt. He was the first to really work at his job and he showed us the way.

Although I didn't know McNamee and was never close to Husing, another radio pioneer was not only a hero to me, but a long-time friend. His name was Bill Munday.

It is difficult today to realize that an announcer could become famous for broadcasting one football game. There are thousands of broadcasts and telecasts every year. Hundreds of capable, well-informed announcers do the broadcasting. Consequently, no matter how talented one may be, no announcer today can make a reputation on the basis of a single broadcast.

In the early days of radio, things were different. That's when my friend Bill Munday came along. He made his reputation on one, single broadcast—the Rose Bowl game of 1929. In those days there was only a small scattering of radio stations across the country. In fact, there weren't even many radios. People stayed up all night, hunched over their crystal sets in a determined effort to move a metal wire (called a cat-whisker) across a blob of mercury and pick Schenectady or Pittsburgh out of the air.

Bill Munday had been a left-handed pitcher for the University of Georgia baseball team. "A left-hander with brains," he used to say. After college days, he joined the sports department of the *Atlanta Journal*, which owned one of the nation's pioneer stations, WSB.

Bill knew his sports. He wrote with the authority of this knowledge, spicing his stories with the idiom of the rural South. He was coming along fine. He was building a local reputation in sports circles and soon won favor of the *Journal* executives. When the paper-owned radio station decided to broadcast the Southern Conference basketball tournament in Atlanta, Bill Munday was the logical choice for announcing duties.

He had never broadcast a sports event before but only a few had. Munday was a confident young man and accepted the assignment with relish. He was a natural. His slangy style made a hit with listeners. He moved to other sports and became—in that early era—the sports voice of the South.

His big chance came January 1, 1929. The Georgia Tech football team swept through the '28 season undefeated to win an invitation to the Rose Bowl, at that time the only bowl game in existence.

Munday worked for the *Atlanta Journal* which owned WSB, a key NBC station. When NBC decided to broadcast the Rose Bowl game coast-to-coast, it asked for Bill Munday. McNamee did the color for that game. Munday and Carl Haverlin shared the play-by-play.

This was a big game and big things happened. Even now—many New Years later—it remains the most famous of all Rose Bowl games, because an 83-yard wrong-way run by California captain Roy Riegels gave Tech an 8–7 victory over Riegels's team.

If the game was famed in sports history, it also made its mark in the annals of broadcasting. On the basis of his performance at the mike for two quarters of that

Rose Bowl game, Bill Munday, the drawling cracker from Georgia, became famous overnight.

His colorful expressions began to dot the conversation of sports fans in other sections of the country. In fact, they are still remembered by many.

"How do you do, ladies and gentlemen of the loud-speaker ensemble," was Munday's salutation.

When a runner was tackled, he was "brought down to terra firma." The end-zone was the "land of milk and honey." To get their signals the teams went into a "crap-shooters' huddle."

Here was the first announcer from the South to hit the network. Since then, there have been many—Mel Allen, Red Barber, Russ Hodges—to name a few. The warmth and informality which Bill Munday brought to that Rose Bowl broadcast survives today.

I remember that Rose Bowl broadcast. It made an impact on me. I was only 10 years old at the time, but Bill Munday became an instant hero to me. He was one of our own who had made good in a big way.

Sports editors hailed his work. Newspapers wrote editorials about his Rose Bowl broadcast. He was a sensation.

NBC hired him for the next several seasons to broadcast football over one of its two networks. In 1929 he took his place alongside McNamee and Husing. Those three were the only announcers on national hookups. In 1930 Bill became the first broadcaster to short-wave a football game outside the United States when NBC (cooperating with the BBC) sent out the Yale-Georgia game from New Haven.

Munday was on top of the world. But the dizzy heights were too much for him.

''I couldn't keep up with those fast-livers,'' he told me later. ''I began to drink and drink heavily.''

All-night bouts with the bottle dulled his reflexes. He lost his job in New York and came back to the *Atlanta Journal*. He lost that job too. Bill became a wanderer of the streets, begging friends for money to buy whiskey. His wife remained loyal. On her way to work, she would drive him into town, bid him goodbye and hope that he got home safely.

That's when I first met Bill Munday. He was begging for quarters and dimes. He was about as far down as anybody could be. I would try to talk with him, but he couldn't comprehend.

Friends found jobs for Bill. One of them came from Niles Trammell, NBC president. He brought Bill back to broadcast an Alabama-Georgia Tech game in Birmingham. But Munday was still drinking. He hit the airwaves with this opening: ''How do you do, ladies and gentlemen of the loudspeaker ensemble. This is Bill Munday from Legion Field in Birmingham, a town of hard drinkers and fast women.'' Before he had a chance to say much else, NBC had jerked Munday off the air.

Later, he was the PA announcer at Ponce de Leon Park in Atlanta for the Cracker games. In my school days I used to sit near him in the press box. He would turn on the mike and you could see his lips move without words coming out. Gradually, words would form and go out over the PA. Again, he didn't last long. Drink kept getting to him.

Soon his health was gone. He also had lost his pride. Doctors gave him only six months to live. Except for his devoted and loyal wife he would have had no clothes on his back, no roof overhead. Then, something happened. Bill Munday found a power greater than himself. God became his manager. That was in 1949. After that, he never touched a drink.

He regained his health. He took a job with the state of Georgia as a public relations director in the fire prevention program. He went back on the air—first on Red Barber's CBS Football Roundup and then as color man on the University of Georgia football network.

In those later years Bill used to visit me in New York. I was broadcasting the Oriole games. He timed his visits to New York when the Baltimore team was playing the Yankees. He loved to go to Yankee Stadium with me and talk with me and others about his career.

"Bill," I told him, "I admire you as much as anybody I've ever met in this business. You were an overnight success and then you crashed. But you came back to win the respect of your friends, your wife, and—most important—of yourself."

He was one of a kind.

I can still hear that drawl and those great expressions. That was Bill Munday.

All of us Southerners have some of Bill Munday in us, consciously or unconsciously. He was a hero of mine in my early years and my entry into radio came somewhat like his—from the newspaper world into the world of radio.

By the time I was a senior at Emory University I had been working for six years on the sports desk of the *Atlanta Constitution*. And I was trying to determine where I might be able to get a job. None was open at the paper.

In my speech class at Emory one of my fellow students was Marcus Bartlett. Older than the rest of us, he was program director at radio station WSB. One spring Saturday morning I was watching an Emory track meet, lolling in the sun in an old pair of pants and a T-shirt.

Mark came up and said hello. "Could you come down to the radio station this afternoon?" he asked.

"Sure," I told him. "I'm going to work at the *Constitution*, but I'll drop in on the way. Should I wear a coat and tie?"

"Yes. I want you to meet my boss."

Knowing no more than that, I went to WSB. When I arrived Mark met me. "Take this sports page," he said. "Go into that studio and read the story of the Cracker game into the mike."

I'd never even been in a radio studio. And certainly had never spoken into a microphone. What I didn't know was that Mark and his boss, Leonard Reinsch, and several other WSB executives were listening. When I finished, Bartlett briefed me. WSB needed a sports man. He had suggested me. The brass liked my reading. Would I return Monday with a 15-minute script based on Sunday's baseball results?

Early Monday morning I came back, took the full audition, and got the job.

I didn't tell them they were hiring an untried youngster who at the age of five had been tongue-tied. But I remembered those early schoolboy days and the taunts about my handicap. I remembered how generous and loving my parents had been to pay for my elocution lessons. How hard those teachers had worked with me and how I had struggled through declamations and debates; and finally in my Emory speech class I must have impressed Marcus Bartlett enough for him to see me as a possibility for that job WSB was now giving me.

* * *

For the next two years—before I enlisted for four in the U.S. Marines—I conducted a nightly program of sports news, comments, and interviews. Bob Jones, Babe Ruth, Jack Dempsey, Don Budge, Ty Cobb, Connie Mack, Charlie Trippi were just some of the sports people I interviewed. I did the color with Bartlett on Georgia Tech football and did pickups on golf, tennis, bowling, and basketball.

One March afternoon in 1941, I was sitting in the cramped newsroom at WSB, chatting with news broadcaster Doug Edwards, when Program Director Mark Bartlett burst into the room with a telegram.

"Ernie!" he shouted. "Big news."

"What?"

"NBC is going to broadcast the Masters and they want you. You'll be working with Bill Stern."

To say I was thrilled would be an understatement— like saying Marie Antoinette died of a sore throat. Stern was the sports king of the industry. NBC was THE network. I'd be doing play-by-play coast-to-coast. This would be my big chance, my first network broadcast.

What I didn't know at the time was the Masters experience would provide me with a personal ultimate in both joy and despair.

Prior to 1942 no national network had ever broadcast the Masters. In its beginnings (it started in 1934) the tournament attracted attention because it marked Bobby Jones's once-a-year emergence from retirement. Radio looked on the event as local, or at best, regional. When I started at WSB in May 1940, that season's tourney was history. The next year the station sent me to Augusta, and I covered not only for WSB, but also for

WWRL, Augusta. Then on the final day, CBS sent Russ Hodges over from their Charlotte affiliate, WBT, for a regional network broadcast.

My new assignment would be different. This time I'd be out on the course following the golfers, doing play-by-play. In '41 I had simply sent back live reports from a tower near the 18th green. Scores, highlights, and interviews—but no play-by-play.

Immediately, I began to prepare for my big chance. Lulu and I lived on Myrtle Street in those days, near the Piedmont golf course. After lunch, Lulu and I would walk to the course. We'd sit behind a green, watch the golfers approach and putt.

"That's blue-shirt," I'd broadcast to her. "He has a 35-foot putt which should break down and to his right."

After the golfers passed, we'd go down to the green and I'd measure the distance—to see how accurate or inaccurate my guess had been.

Another part of my preparation was a visit to the home of O. B. (Pop) Keeler, the internationally famous golf writer for the *Atlanta Journal*. He had covered every tournament that Bobby Jones had entered. Every Bobby Jones book had been written by O. B. He also wrote the movie short subjects in which Jones appeared. And when he covered the British Open in 1930 (when Jones achieved his famous Grand Slam), Keeler became the first broadcaster of a sports event from overseas. O. B. was Mr. Big among golf writers of the world.

O. B. (everybody called him Pop) lived with Mrs. Keeler (everybody called her Mama) in a cozy little home he called Distillery Hill in his by-line column. Mama was a golf writer too. She covered the ladies' events. Pop Keeler greeted me warmly and ushered me into the sun room. Mama was seated in a corner, knitting a sweater.

"Pop, I'm going to broadcast the Masters on NBC," I told him. "I know a little about golf—about as much as the average sportscaster—and I want to be fully prepared."

"No problem, Ernie," he told me. "I'll be more than happy to help you."

So we sat there and chatted about golf in general and the Masters in particular. All the time, Mama Keeler was silently knitting in the corner.

Finally she interrupted.

"O. B.," she said. "I don't understand. Do you mean to tell me that a national network is broadcasting this big event, the Masters, and they're using a young boy just a couple of years out of school and who has never broadcast a golf tournament in his life? I can't believe it!"

"Mama," said O. B. "Don't worry about it."

Then he turned toward me and put his hand on my knee.

"Son," he asked, "can you count?"

"Yes, sir."

"Then broadcasting the Masters will be no problem for you. You'll do fine."

He was right. The broadcast did go well. Stern worked out of a tower. He used two announcers, Bob Stanton, a network veteran out of New York, and me. Stanton and I followed the golfers. Stern would feed scores from the tower, and we would break in over our remote units from points around the course. Our remote equipment on the world's largest network would be ridiculed today. Each announcer had an engineer with a bicycle on which a small transmitter was mounted. As we followed the golfers, the engineer and I would push through the crowds and try to pick a high spot so that our transmitters would reach the tower.

The equipment was primitive, but it worked. Stern was happy with my description and so was NBC. I really didn't see a whole lot of Stern. He was pleasant enough but ignored me unless he wanted me to do something for him. He had a writer-producer named Jack Dillon whom he ran ragged. Bill was very demanding, and when he said "Jump!", Jack Dillon jumped. Also, with his wooden leg, Stern didn't move around too well, so that put an extra burden on Dillon.

I was happy. I was network, and I could see the difference in the reaction of the people who ran the Masters. The year before I had been just a kid from an Atlanta station. Indeed, that first year when Hodges came down from CBS on the final day, the folks who had been nice to me suddenly ignored me for Hodges. But now I was *NBC*, and they seemed to feel differently toward me.

So, my big chance came. And went.

When I returned home, there were compliments.

"Hey, I heard you on the Masters. Nice job."

"Glad you made the network, Ernie."

Still, nothing more than that. It was a letdown. NBC didn't call with any big offers. My life really hadn't changed. Anyway, the war was accelerating, and soon I'd be in the service. People had other things to think about.

Within three months, I was in Marine bootcamp at Parris Island. The Masters, Bill Stern, and NBC were all behind me. I pushed aside that memory as I worried about a clean rifle, a starched uniform, and survival in the Marines.

The longest, slowest four years in my life followed. Then, in 1946, I was back from overseas and finally out of the USMC.

Discharged in January, I returned to WSB.

"You can have the old job back," John Outlar, the station manager told me. "But we don't have room for your sports show. Too much network programming. We can put you on for five minutes each night after the 11 o'clock news."

"No thanks," I told him. "I think I'd rather free-lance. I want to do play-by-play."

"You're making a mistake," Outlar told me. "There are only four stations in Atlanta—all network. They won't have room for baseball or any other sports."

So, I decided to free-lance anyway. My eyes were on the Atlanta Cracker broadcast job, and, I told myself, I could supplement that with a show on another station. And maybe other jobs.

I sat down and wrote Bill Stern at NBC asking if he could use me again on the Masters.

He wrote back and said yes. "It will be wonderful to work with you again," he wrote me. "See you in Augusta."

Meanwhile, I was visiting the military hospitals around the South, showing sports movies for Chesterfield and handing out free copies of *The Sporting News*. Also, I arranged with *Holiday* magazine to write an article on the Masters.

I studied the newspaper files for information on previous Masters and prepared myself for working on NBC again with Bill Stern.

When I reported to Stern at Augusta, he gave me a jolt.

"This time we're going to use a different system," he told me. "You'll still be out on the course with a walkie-talkie and an engineer, but this year instead of you calling in, I will be in the tower, and I'll switch to you on my cue."

I didn't like the new system. I could see problems in it. But, after all, I was only working for Stern—not running the show. When Stern worked, he ran the show, and nobody else even tried.

Our first broadcast was Saturday. Stern pulled me aside for instructions.

"You will pick up Bob Jones and Lawson Little at the second green and describe the play. I'll open the show at the tower. I'll keep it one minute and then switch to you for your stroke-by-stroke description. No matter what happens, you stay on the air three minutes and then switch back to me at the tower."

My engineer and I headed for the second green, pushing the bike and its walkie-talkie. We set up and waited. Broadcast time arrived.

Over our earphones we heard Stern sign on. What a great dramatic voice he had! We held our stop watches and eyed the hand as it moved around. Meanwhile, Jones and Little had reached the second green and were putting. Stern was still talking past the self-allotted one minute. The hand went around and around again and still again. More than three minutes had passed. Still no cue for me to begin. Stern was still indulging himself in his opening remarks.

Now Little and Jones had left the second green. They were teeing off on the third hole. Just after each had hit his tee shots, I heard Stern give me the cue, "And now to the second green and Ernie Harwell."

The second green was there. Ernie Harwell was there. But the golfers had gone. Jones and Little were walking down the third fairway with a large gallery at their heels. The second green was deserted—just an engineer, bicycle, and I were still there.

Nobody and nothing. Still I must talk. ("No matter what happens," he had said, "keep it a full three minutes.") I started: "Jones and Little passed here and were even after two holes. They have driven off the third tee. We'll try to catch them and describe their shots."

I began to run, sounding like a Whirlaway, rounding the turn. The words came hard, on heavy breath. Finally, engineer, bicycle and Harwell pushed through the gallery to the third green. I described the putts on that green.

It was a poor job. I knew it. Stern had run overtime, switched late, and I had nothing to talk about. After I walked back to the tower, Stern excoriated me.

"Why didn't you fake it?" he demanded. "Nobody would have known the difference."

Then he showed me how.

"You should have said, 'Here we are at the third tee. There goes Jones's tee shot down the middle.' This is show business, kid. Don't worry about what really happened."

"I don't work that way," I answered.

"And listen," he said. "You could have stopped Jones and Little. Held 'em up for an interview. You could have told them they were on NBC."

In those days, such behavior wasn't tolerated in golf tournaments. Things have changed, and now the TV networks and tournaments work together differently. But in 1946, I stood in awe of Bob Jones and Lawson Little and the Masters. It was unthinkable for anyone to interfere with the play of the tournament.

"Bill," I said, "I couldn't do that. I can't stop golfers in the middle of a tournament. If you want an announcer to do that, you'll have to get somebody else."

"Alright," he shouted. "I'm giving you another chance. Go out and follow Hogan and Nelson."

"I will, but I'm not stopping any golfers. I'm not faking a hole either."

This time Stern sent another announcer with me and the engineer. When we got to the eighth green, Stern called over the walkie-talkie.

"Ernie," he said, "let the other guy announce."

My heart sank. I headed back to the tower.

"This is all for me, Bill," I told him. "I'm going home."

"Okay," said Stern. "That's fine with me. The trouble with you, Ernie, is that you're too much of a gentleman. Because of that, you'll never get anywhere in radio."

I went home to Atlanta.

My world had caved in. I knew I was through. Everybody in American would know I had failed.

But did they? There was nothing in the paper about the broadcast. A few friends told me they heard me. Some said I'd done a fine job. Others simply said they heard the broadcast. Nobody mentioned that I had been a flop . . . they just didn't seem to pay that much attention.

Flying home, I'd thought about quitting radio. I could write. I could work on a newspaper. I could do something. But after I had heard those comments, I realized that nobody really pays attention. My lesson was a hard one but I had learned it.

Now I was ready to try again—on another broadcast. I would prove to myself that I could get the job done.

Years later—after I had reached New York and was working there in radio—I used to see Stern once in a while. He was always pleasant enough and even interviewed me on his show. The Masters had been forgotten by both of us.

But those two tournaments—one which went so well and one which didn't—taught me one of my many lessons in the world of sports broadcasting.

All the time I was at WSB, I dreamed of doing baseball play-by-play. That was my first love.

I listened as often as I could to baseball announcers. I heard the major leaguers only on All-Star Games or World Series, but most every night I could tune in Joe Hill, who did the Cracker games on WAGA.

My heroes then were Mel Allen, Red Barber, and Bob Elson. I listened carefully to them and envied them in their big league jobs.

Later I got to know these three and to appreciate them on a personal basis. I even had the privilege of working with Red for one full year and part of another.

When I went to Brooklyn for my first big league job in mid-season of 1948, Red was in the hospital recovering from a perforated ulcer attack. I worked with Connie Desmond until Red returned to duty. He came back for a Dodger night game at the Polo Grounds,

September 9, 1948. Red wasn't feeling well and the three of us shared the mike. Rex Barney, the Dodger right-hander, made it a memorable occasion by pitching a no-hitter and blanking the Giants, 2–0. It was the first game I had ever worked with Barber.

The one quality which impressed you about Red Barber was his professionalism. He had great pride in his performance and never settled for second best. He was alert and he always prepared himself thoroughly for every game. Red was a perfectionist and he demanded the best, not only from himself, but also from those with whom he worked.

This striving sometimes made for tenuous moments in the booth. Sometimes Barber would become over-demanding. He was especially harsh on our young statistician, Bob Pasotti. Bob had to carry Number One pencils for Red for the day games and Number Two pencils for the night games. He also had to bring along a portable lamp for Red because many of the booths in the away parks weren't lighted adequately for the Ole Redhead.

If things went wrong, sometimes Red would hurl a pencil or a scorebook in the direction of young Pasotti. Bob became proficient at dodging. He had a lot of practice.

Barber was really two different people. On the air he projected the image of a laid-back, good ole Southern charmer. It was "I'll be a suck-egg mule;" or, "He's sitting in the catbird seat;" or, "Don't you go 'way, ya heah."

Off the air, he was serious and introspective. He was intense and sometimes if you said something he wanted to challenge, he would look right through you with a set of piercing eyes.

On one of our 1949 trips, most of us in the Dodger traveling party had to double-up in the rooms at the Stevens hotel in Chicago. Red and I were paired. As I waited for him to get ready to go out to dinner I looked across Michigan Boulevard and saw two bums, lying on the grass.

"Look at that," I said in an attempt at small talk. "Those two guys lying out there in the sun. No cares, no problems. Whatta life!"

"Oh, no. You're all wrong, Ernie," was Red's retort. "Those two men are derelicts. They've wasted their lives. More than likely they've deserted their wives and children. Also, they're now living off society. Certainly, we shouldn't admire people like that. Maybe we can pity them, but they are doing a great disservice to themselves, to those who love them, and to all of mankind."

Yet, the next day in the radio booth at Wrigley Field, Red would appear on the air to be as loose as ashes, joking with me about my native state of Georgia or some other bit which he had picked up for that purpose.

Desmond and Barber worked well together on the air. But Connie did not like Red. I think Barber was more tolerant of Desmond than vice-versa, and he certainly was more careful and discreet when he talked about Connie than Connie was in his conversations about Red.

Often I was caught in the middle.

I remember an incident from my first season, 1948. Barber was still in the hospital and Connie and I were broadcasting the games. Before a game at Brooklyn, one of the agency men (from Young & Rubicam, I believe) delivered the commercials for the broadcast. They had been written for Barber before Red's illness. And they were couched in the famous Barber lingo—deep South-slanted with all the Barberisms possible. Connie gave a quick look and saw how the commercials were worded.

"Forget it," he shouted. Then he took the script and threw it toward the back of the booth. "If they think I'm another 'ole Redhead', they're all wrong. Why don't they write this damn stuff in English?"

On the air there was never any evidence of strife between Red and Connie. Both were outstanding announcers. Red was always number one but Connie could have been tops on any broadcast team. I'm sure that Desmond dreamed of the time when he would be the number one Dodger announcer. But in those years there was never any indication that Red would ever move from the job. He was an institution.

When Barber went to the Yankees, it surprised all of us. Connie then inherited the number one spot. But he lasted only a few years. He started to drink heavily and lost the job. One theory was that he increased his drinking because of the pressure of the number one spot— the job he had coveted for so long. When it came to him, it was too much for him to handle.

I know that when I worked with Red and Connie, Connie was a social drinker. It didn't go beyond that. Later, his drinking was such a problem that he could not hold the job. Walter O'Malley fired him once. Then Connie joined AA and came back. Still, he couldn't hang on. The booze got to him again.

"I can't make it, Walter," he told O'Malley. "Thanks for giving me that second shot. But I just can't stay off the stuff."

Connie was through—left to the streets. Later I would see him in the hotel lobby when I came to New York. We'd visit and he'd take a "loan" and go on his way.

He didn't have to drink to reinforce himself. He was an outstanding announcer, good enough to succeed Red or anyone else. Maybe it was something else that projected him into that disaster.

He was good to me. When I first reported to work with him he was generous and kind and helpful.

I think Red appreciated Connie as a partner, too. Red wanted the best and he knew that a broadcast team is never stronger than its weakest link.

Barber's approach to baseball was like Husing's. He was thorough and incisive. If Husing was the first announcer ever really to make a study of football, Red was the same kind of pioneer in baseball. He was the first to do all the little things which solid preparation requires. We take these things for granted today (most all announcers do them), but Red was the first.

I would come to the booth and say, "Erskine's not feeling well today."

"Why not?" Red would ask. "Did you talk with him? Or, did somebody else tell you?"

Red himself would check out the players, umpires, trainers, and managers. Nothing slipped past him. He was great at spotting pitchers warming up in the bullpens. His eyes were sharp and he had an outstanding memory bank for different pitching motions and other characteristics.

Barber was excellent on explaining strategy to his listeners. He knew the options a manager might have and was very discerning about the inside points of the game. His theory was to broadcast the ball. He reported the action and let the color of the game fall into place afterward. He was a master and I was fortunate to work with him and to learn from him.

I didn't always feel comfortable around Red. After all, in previous years he had been my idol and hero. It was difficult for me to look on myself as a co-worker. Also, he was often cool and stand-offish in his personal relationships—not the warm and relaxed Red Barber the Dodger fans had depicted from years of listening to him.

I'm sure Vin Scully, who replaced me in Brooklyn, must have had the same feelings about Red in his early days of working with him. Right after Vin was hired by the Dodgers in the winter of 1949, I invited him to dinner at my Larchmont home. I discussed my job with the Dodgers and tried to give him some insight about the situations which might arise for him.

Later in his first season, we met again.

"The 'ole Redhead's' giving me a tough time," he told me.

"Just hang in there," I said. "He's tough, but he's a great teacher. It'll be worth it."

It was strange the way my path and Scully's path began to cross.

Vin had worked on campus radio at Fordham. The summer after he graduated in 1949 he interned at WTOP in Washington. When fall arrived, that job was over and he came home to New Jersey. He visited CBS one afternoon for a job interview with Barber.

"I was impressed by Scully. But we had no job openings at the time. I didn't even get his name," Red recalled.

Red's main focus at that time was on the CBS football

roundup. His regular announcers on this sports round-robin were Connie Desmond and I. Others were recruited for weekly duty. The Chicago sports writer Warren Brown always covered Notre Dame.

One Saturday Warren couldn't make the Notre Dame-North Carolina game at Yankee Stadium, the number one matchup of that week's schedule. So, Barber shifted me from the Boston University-Maryland game to the Irish-Tarheel battle.

Now, he had to find someone to replace me. He remembered Scully and the impression he'd made. Red tracked him down and assigned him to the game in Boston.

It was bitter cold, but Vin, working with a hand mike on the stadium roof, did an excellent job.

Several weeks later I decided to leave the Dodger broadcasting team and go to the Giants. Again, Red looked to Scully as my replacement and hired Vince to join his Dodger broadcast. So, for the first time within a month, Scully replaced Harwell.

Vin has been with the Dodgers ever since. He has done an outstanding job over the years and is generally regarded as the premiere baseball announcer.

I left Brooklyn with regrets. It had been great fun there and I had worked with top-notch people. My new partner with the Giants, Russ Hodges, had a different approach than Barber. He was more relaxed and less of a perfectionist than the "ole Redhead."

"I want you to have fun over here," was his first greeting to me. "There'll just be two of us working radio and TV. We'll do a good job, but we'll enjoy it, too."

Sandlot Scene in Atlanta, 1931. L to R: Ernie,
Billy Carter, Earl Dolive.

Ernie interviewing Ted
Williams on WSB-
Atlanta in 1942.

Lulu and Sgt. Ernie
Harwell in Atlanta,
1943.

Ponce de Leon Park, Atlanta, GA, 1948. L to R: Kiki Cuyler, Mike Benton (WBGE owner), Earl Mann (Atlanta Crackers owner), Gov. M.E. Thompson, Ernie, Maurice Coleman (WBGE manager), and Frank Russell (Old Gold).

L to R: Ernie, Red Barber, and Connie Desmond in Brooklyn, 1949.

Visiting the Vets in 1950. L to R: Al Dark, Whitey Lockman, Ernie, and Sal Maglie.

Above: Sportswriter Barney Kremenko, Bobby Thomson, and Ernie talking about Bobby's famous home run in 1952. *Below:* Ernie chats with Connie Mack, Home Run (Frank) Baker, and Art Ehlers in Baltimore in the mid-'50s.

Russ Hodges and Ernie at the Polo Grounds, New York, 1950.

Below: Ernie watches Oriole manager Jimmy Dykes sink a putt in Yuma, AZ, 1954.

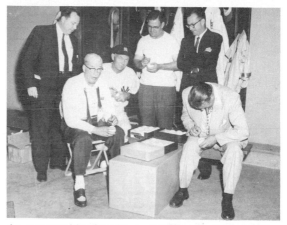

An autographing session in Baltimore in the mid-'50s.
L to R: Paul Welch, Lefty Grove, Bill Dickey, Mel Ott,
Ernie, and Jimmy Foxx.

On the links in Baltimore, 1955. L to R: Chuck
Thompson, Ernie, Bailey Goss, Jack Dunn.

Ernie introduces Ty Cobb at Baltimore Memorial Stadium, 1957.

An Arizona visit in 1962 with the founder of *The Sporting News*. L to R: Lulu Harwell, Blanche Spink, Ernie, and J.G. Taylor Spink.

Ernie with Denny McLain and Ray Lane in Detroit, 1968.

Ernie talking to the NY Yankees in Baseball Chapel at Tiger Stadium, 1979. *Photo: J.D. McCarthy*

Five Hall of Famers, 1983. L to R: Charlie Gehringer, George Kell, Hank Greenberg, Ernie, and Al Kaline. *Photo: Bill Eisner*

Ernie and Tiger Manager Sparky Anderson ready for another season in 1985.

Russ had a certain reserved respect for Barber, but was certainly not fond of him. He told me a story of a football game they had broadcast together.

"Red did the first quarter of the game," he said. "When he'd finished he introduced me to the radio audience, saying 'Now for the second quarter, here is Russ Hughes.' "

"I came right back at him. 'Thank you, Red Baker,' I said, and went right into my play-by-play."

Where Barber was the consummate baseball reporter, Russ Hodges was Everyman. Russ was the guy next door, or the guy in the bar telling you in very simple, straightforward terms what was happening on the field. He was probably a better football announcer and a better boxing announcer than Red. But Barber, I felt, was much superior to Hodges in baseball.

Russ was a social person. He enjoyed a drink, good food, and a party. He was a very sharp businessman and could always call on his many friends when he needed them.

Russ had come to the Giants from the Yankees the year before I arrived at the Polo Grounds. He had worked with Mel Allen for three years and I think that association has contributed to his relaxed outlook on broadcasting. It taught him that the broadcast wasn't everything in life. Allen, like Barber, approached his job with sheer intensity.

"The problem with Melvin," Russ used to say, "is that baseball is his whole life. He's not married. He has no wife to worry about. No kids with chicken pox or measles. All he is concerned about is whether he'll broadcast the next All-Star Game or the World Series. He has all his eggs in one emotional basket."

So, Russ and I had a relaxing time. The Giants were not as good a team as the Dodgers. But Leo Durocher was much more interesting than Burt Shotton, the Brooklyn manager. And Willie Mays, Sal Maglie, Eddie Stanky, Al Dark, and the other Giants were a great bunch to travel with.

Swapping Barber for Hodges as a partner had a touch of irony. When I replaced Red in August 1948, it was because he had been felled by an ulcer. Soon after my landing the Giant job, Russ came down with an ailment which threatened to end his announcing career. He didn't reach a near-death status as Barber did; but he was certainly deeply worried about his future.

At first Russ thought he'd had a stroke. But it was Bell's Palsy. It happened in late November of 1949. Hodges broadcast the Columbia-Navy football game in the bitter cold at Annapolis. Snow which had begun at halftime, was a blizzard by the time Russ reached New York. He struggled home to Tuckahoe, New York, cold, wet and exhausted.

"About two in the morning," he later recalled, "I got up for some water. I filled the glass, brought it to my lips, but only a little dribble went down my throat. The rest slobbered down my neck and over my pajamas.

"I thought I'd had a stroke. The right side of my face had collapsed. I couldn't move my mouth. I couldn't close my right eye. I tried to speak. Only a slight mumble came out."

The next day Russ contacted Dr. Harrison McLaughlin. Dr. McLaughlin told Russ that when he heard of the symptoms he had feared a stroke, but now thought that Russ had Bell's Palsy.

"It's caused by the pinching of a facial nerve, usually due to extreme cold," he explained to Russ. "There might always be a slight facial deformity, but there won't be any other permanent damage. You could go back to work in about six months."

Even before spring training, Russ was well again. Rest and deep-heat therapy had readied him for our first season together. Yet, he did have a scare.

Together we had another scare, but this was a humorous one.

I don't remember during which of our four seasons this happened, but I do recall that it happened on a hot Sunday afternoon. Our booth at the Polo Grounds was hung down from the upper deck. It was cramped and very difficult to get in and out of. In those days when Russ and I broadcast a doubleheader, we also did a between-game show on TV.

"I hate this little, cramped booth," Russ used to say. "And the worst part is, there's no toilet. We have to go to the public rest rooms, if at all."

To alleviate our relief problems, we decided to make use of large paper cups. Out of the sight of anybody, we would urinate into the cups and then put the cups on the floor of the booth.

This hot Sunday afternoon, some visitor to the booth kicked over one of the cups. The amber fluid spilled over the floor and leaked through the boards onto the box seat patrons down below.

Soon Barney O'Toole, the head usher at the Polo Grounds appeared in our booth.

"Hey, you guys," he said, "we're getting complaints from those people in the box seats. They said for you to quit spilling beer on 'em."

"Barney," I told him, "if it's beer, it's used beer. We'll be careful, but don't tell those folks what really hit 'em."

Toward the end of the 1950 season, my first with the Giants, Russ came to me with a surprise.

"How would you feel about doing the Red Sox games?" he asked.

"I just don't know" was my answer.

"Well," Russ continued, "Tom Yawkey is a good friend of mine. He knows about you and likes your work. He asked me if you'd like to come to Boston and be his broadcaster."

I thought about it and within a week had my answer.

I turned down the Boston offer. My reason was that I had been in Brooklyn a year and half and with the Giants for only one season. I felt that I didn't want to move my family again and also didn't want to get the reputation of an announcer jumping from job to job every year.

So, I stayed with the Giants. Curt Gowdy, who had worked that 1950 season with the Yankees, became the Red Sox announcer.

I always thought that Gowdy, while he was doing all sports for NBC-TV, was the best all-around in the business. He was excellent on basketball (the sport he had played) and just as good on baseball and football. He always turned in a professional performance.

Curt and I worked together twice on the CBS radio broadcast of the American League playoffs. He proved to be an able partner and a delightful man with whom to work.

When I left the Giants for Baltimore, I had a chance to hook up with another talented broadcaster—Chuck

Thompson. My first-year partners were Bailey Goss and Howie Williams. But in 1955 Chuck replaced Howie. Thompson has a magnificent voice and delivery. He always reminds me of Ted Husing. We worked both the Orioles and the football Colts together.

One of the booster clubs for the Colts staged a banquet which Chuck and I attended. After the dinner, one of the Colt fans button-holed Chuck.

"You're not pronouncing Syzmanski's name right," he told Thompson. "You're saying 'Sis-manski.' It should be pronounced 'Syz-manski.' "

"Thank you very much," Chuck said.

"That's okay," the fan replied. "And tell that Ernie Hardwell, too."

We had a change of beer sponsors in 1956. So, the following year I switched breweries and stayed on baseball. Chuck stayed with the brewery and broadcast football. The switch brought me a new partner, Herb Carneal. It was Herb's first big league job. He was outstanding from the start; low-key with a wry sense of humor and a good feel for the game. We had a good working arrangement and I hated to leave him when I went to Detroit for the 1960 season.

At Detroit, I replaced Van Patrick who had broadcast the Tigers for eight years. Patrick was bitter about my replacing him, but as time went by, his bitterness lessened. I wanted to keep my friendship with Van. I had known him from his early years of Tiger broadcasting. We used to visit each other's homes and often ate out together. I enjoyed his company.

Once in Baltimore, Lulu and I had a party for the Tiger traveling media group. Jack Tighe, the Tiger manager, secretary Charlie Creedon, the newspapermen, Patrick and his broadcasting partner Mel Ott—all came to my house to eat Maryland crabs. Patrick ate 24 steamed crabs. And my nephew, Rhee Harwell, only about 3 at the time, bit a hunk out of Mel Ott's leg.

Van was sensitive to fan letters. On one of my trips to Briggs Stadium, he pulled me aside. He took out a newspaper clipping and showed it to me.

"Can you imagine this?" he asked. "Look how this letterwriter put the blast on me."

He'd been carrying that clipping around for several weeks.

"I wouldn't worry about it," I told him. "All of us get that kind of reaction once in a while."

"But this guy keeps writing the newspapers, calling me 'ole flannel mouth.' I'm going to do something about it."

Van's partner, George Kell, told me later what Van did.

Patrick hired a private detective to trace the writer of the anonymous letters. When he found the writer's name, address and phone number, he started a campaign against him.

Suddenly coal was delivered to the letterwriter's house. Unordered packages came from Hudson's and other department stores. The letterwriter's phone began to ring at odd hours and the voices of young ladies would ask his wife if he were home. He was thoroughly harassed.

Patrick's revenge worked.

"I've had enough," his one-time tormentor wrote. "If you'll call off the dogs, I won't write any more letters about you."

You had to admire Patrick as a fighter. Right up until the day he died, he fought the cancer that killed him. In the fall of 1974 he was dying, but continued to broadcast both the Lions and the Notre Dame football games. He worked as long as he possibly could. On Friday, September 27, Van did his last show, taping a pre-game interview with Notre Dame coach Ara Parseghian. Mutual aired the interview before the Irish-Purdue game the next afternoon.

However, Patrick never made it to the stadium. He became ill Saturday morning and was rushed to a South Bend hospital. He died Sunday afternoon about the time his other team, the Lions, received the kickoff from the Packers at Green Bay.

Van had followed two much-loved Detroit baseball broadcasters—Harry Heilmann and Ty Tyson. Even today, I hear praise for these two. I never knew Heilmann. I was in the National League in his final years. He died in Detroit in 1951, the night before the All-Star Game at Briggs Stadium.

It's been said (I've never been able to confirm it) that Ty Cobb visited Harry the day he died and told him untruthfully that he had been elected to the Baseball Hall of Fame. Harry was named to the Hall of Fame, but his election came a year after his death.

I knew Tyson. He was retired and living in Grosse Pointe. Often, I would pick him up and drive him to the Tiger games. He was sharp-witted and a keen observer. One of my most popular broadcasts was on Father's Day when I put Ty on the air and he broadcast an inning of a Tiger game. All of his fans were delighted to hear him again.

Through my years in Detroit I've been blessed with

great partners—George Kell, Bob Scheffing, Gene Osborn, Ray Lane, and Paul Carey. Each one has been special to me. In radio-TV booths across the country, I've spent more time with these guys than with my own family. Together we've sweltered in the summer heat and frozen in early April and late September. In sickness and in health, we've been together. And we've seen some bizarre things in those booths.

One day at Tiger Stadium, George Kell and I had a visit from the mayor of a small Michigan city. His visit was prompted by the cheese festival which his city was sponsoring. He had come to present George and me with a large wheel of cheese encased in a circle of heavy wood. In those days the only entry to our booth was through a hatch in the middle of a slanted roof. The mayor had been drinking and he was very shaky. Holding the large wheel of cheese, he tried to maneuver himself down the hatch and into our booth. He slipped. The cheese hit the slanted roof and rolled off the edge. It tumbled below into the crowded box seats, just missing an eight-year-old boy. If it had hit the youngster, it could have killed him.

When Ray Lane was my partner, a man about 20 years old slipped by the usher and came to the door of our booth. I went to the door to greet him.

"Hi," he said. "I'm Mickey Cochrane's nephew. He told me to tell you hello."

"Is that right!" I answered. "How is Uncle Mickey?"

"Oh, he's doing fine."

That was 1970. Mickey Cochrane had died in 1962.

I've been very fortunate to work in Detroit. The Tiger fans are knowledgeable. Their devotion to baseball is handed down from one generation to the next. Also, they are aware of the lore, tradition and the history of the game.

The people of Detroit have always been loyal to their radio and TV sports announcers. They have given me warmth and affection far beyond what I deserve. I've had a strong, powerful station behind me in WJR. The station and the Tigers have been supportive power-houses. No announcer could ask for more.

Over the years, I've seen quite a variety of sportscasters. Anyone who has been around them for a while can tell you that a sportscaster is a strange creature.

From 200 feet, he can identify the pitch as a slider on the outside corner; but he can't tell you the color of his wife's eyes.

He can paint a glowing word picture of the San Gabriel mountains past the rim of the Rose Bowl; but when he goes to the hardware store, he is always asking for one of those thing-a-ma-jigs that will fit into a whatcha-ma-call-it.

He's a reporter, entertainer, salesman, teacher, orator, and philosopher. Others would murder to get a ticket to the game, but the sportscaster gets in free and has the best seat in the stadium. And, every fan knows that broadcasting a game is the easiest job in the world.

As a kid shortstop, the sportscaster couldn't stop a grapefruit from rolling uphill, but he can tell three million listeners that Alan Trammell should have played that last hitter at least five steps to the left.

He gets letters, too; some are kind—the rest he turns over to the FBI. One lady writes: "I want you to go away with me.'' Another lady writes: ''I want you to go away.''

He always remembers his daughter's birthday. Easy . . . it was the night of the first Ali-Frazier fight. And he can memorize the uniform numbers of 55 players on a college football team, but he can't recall at which dry cleaners he left his dirty shirts.

A sportscaster likes action-packed games, hot coffee, big excited crowds, friendly press rooms, loyal fans, and free food and drink. He dislikes doubleheaders, freezing football weather, rain delays, and mumbling athletes who punctuate every three words with ''you know, you know, you know.''

A sportscaster goes on a 17-day trip. On the night he returns home his mouth is watering for a home-cooked meal. So, the whole family insists on eating at the fanciest restaurant in town.

On that rare day off, he doesn't feel well enough to mow the lawn. Besides, he has to play 36 holes of golf that afternoon.

He dresses like Woody Allen, talks like Mel Allen, and his wife looks like Steve Allen.

The sportscaster can smooth-talk a worldwide Super Bowl audience, but at the PTA meeting he is tongue-tied.

His fans love him, the athletes tolerate him and his family calls him Daddy.

Looking back, he realizes it's been a good life.
He's seen the stars in action . . .
From Jimmy Brown to Reggie Jackson,
Elvin Hayes and Willie Mays,
Roger Maris and Bucky Harris.

As he narrates their parade,
Wondering if it's just charade.
He can be vindictive or forgiving,
For all the games that he saw played.
Remember, now, he never paid.
And, he must admit that all of it
Beats working for a living!

6

Everybody's Human

A BLOOPER ON THE AIR IS FUN FOR EVERYBODY, EX-cept the guy who makes it. The announcer is cha-grined and embarrassed. He sometimes has to live with his mistake for an entire career.

All of us have pulled our share of bloopers. Some of them have been hilarious. Others have been simply stu-pid mistakes. Our audiences seem to enjoy them, even if we announcers don't.

My number one boo-boo came in a Tiger-Angel game at Anaheim on August 30, 1976. Steve Crawford was pitching in relief for the Tigers. With the score tied, 1-1, in the eighth inning, Angel runner Dave Collins decided to steal home. He dashed from third toward the plate. Crawford delivered the pitch. Collins slid and was called safe by Umpire Rich Garcia.

"He's safe," I told the radio audience. "Collins has slid in safely with the tie-breaking run. But there'll be an argument. Here comes Tiger manager Ralph Houk.

He's steaming. Bill Freehan is there too. Now Freehan is beating his meat at home plate. I mean, beating his mitt at home plate.''

The mail? Honestly, I didn't get a letter or a phone call of protest. Maybe it was because the Tigers were doing so badly. The defeat dropped them 19 games out of first place. Or it might have been the lateness of the hour. When Collins dashed home, it was almost 2 a.m. in Detroit.

The former Pittsburgh Pirate announcer Bob Prince broadcast an exhibition game in which he lost a shortstop. The Pirates stopped over in Memphis on their way north from spring training. The old ballpark there, Russwood Park, had a humpback diamond. There was a drastic slope down from the infield toward the outfield. The Pittsburgh shortstop was Clem Koshorek, sometimes called Scooter. Clem was only 5 feet, 6 inches tall.

An opposing batter lifted a pop fly into short left field. Here's what Bob Prince said:

There's a pop-up into short left. Here comes Kiner in to try for it. Koshorek is going back into left field. The ball may drop in. Koshorek has disappeared. Where in the hell is Koshorek?''

There have been slips of the tongue even on World Series broadcasts. In 1959 Byrum Saam, who broadcast baseball for 38 years in Philadelphia, was working the World Series with Mel Allen. Allen had finished his stint of broadcasting the first four and a half innings of a game between the Dodgers and the White Sox. It was his duty to turn the mike over to Saam for the rest of the game.

''Now, ladies and gentlemen, to bring you along for

the rest of the way, it's my pleasure to introduce to you a man who has broadcast many years of baseball in Philadelphia. He's Byrum Saam, an accurate, colorful, exciting announcer.''

Saam grabbed the mike and absent-mindedly said: "That's right, Mel.''

Red Barber, emceeing his CBS ''Football Roundup'' once made an introduction he regretted. It was almost time for the network station break cue, but Red felt he could get in one more quick report. So, he took a chance. ''Now,'' he said, ''we'll switch to Knoxville, Tennessee and Bingo Blanchard to report the Tennessee-Alabama game. But, Bingo, take no more than 20 seconds because we're coming up on the network cue.''

Well, you know what happened. Bingo could not keep that report within 20 seconds. He ran on for a minute and 35 seconds.

''And now back to Red Barber,'' he concluded.

''Well, son,'' snipped the 'ole Redhead,' ''I think we'll send you a watch for Christmas.''

Red told me that when he was broadcasting the Red games in Cincinnati in the '30s, he had the wrong Cincinnati third baseman play the entire game. That gives us all encouragement. If it can happen to a real pro like Barber, we don't have to feel so bad about our own mistakes.

Mel Allen had his turn when he broadcast a Yankee game at Cleveland in 1963. It was the first game of a Sunday doubleheader. The Indians were scheduled to pitch Sam McDowell in the first game and Jack Kralick in the second. Manager Birdie Tebbetts decided to change and use Kralick in the first game.

The Yankee statistician Bill Kane had given the Yankees' announcers—Allen, Jerry Coleman, and Phil Rizzuto—the first lineup, which listed McDowell as the Indian pitcher.

The game started and Mel Allen was talking about McDowell and his motion and the way he was mowing down the Yankee hitters. Coleman and Rizzuto went right along with him. Finally, a fan called the press box in the fifth inning and talked to Bill Kane. He went to Rizzuto.

"Hey, Phil," he said, "that's Kralick pitching . . . not McDowell."

Rizzuto, who was on the radio, made the correction. But Kane still hadn't told Allen. Finally, he got up enough courage to break the news to Mel. At first Allen didn't believe it. He kept saying McDowell was pitching. Later, he switched and admitted that the Indian pitcher indeed was Kralick.

The amazing part of that fiasco was that the TV station personnel—both in Cleveland and in New York—didn't catch the boo-boo. Both the pitchers were left-handers, but they had different mannerisms and pitching form. And they had different numbers on their uniforms.

In the 1950s the Phillies had an excellent broadcaster named Gene Kelly. He was an intense, hard-working announcer. He also was devoted to baseball. He ate, slept and lived it.

Just before a night game in 1957 at old Shibe Park, somebody told Kelly that Joe McCarthy had died. Kelly was on the air just moments later with a long, flowery tribute to the long-time baseball manager. He recalled how McCarthy, who never played in a major league game, had led the Cubs to a pennant in 1929, switched to the Yankees and won eight pennants there. He related how McCarthy had managed the Red Sox his final three seasons, coming close but never winning.

Kelly proceeded through five minutes of accolades for McCarthy and then took a commercial break. The phone in the booth rang.

"Gene," said a voice from the studio. "That was a great tribute. But you had the wrong McCarthy. The one who died was *Senator* Joe McCarthy."

A Bob Elson blooper was promulgated in Chicago by Bob's good friend and rival broadcaster, Jack Brickhouse. Bob and Jack were broadcasting a White Sox game to their respective stations. Over a season or two Elson had gotten into the habit of listening to Brickhouse in the next booth, picking up tidbits from Jack and passing them along to his own audience.

"I'll fix that Elson," Brickhouse told himself.

One afternoon Jack cut off his microphone and said in a tone so loud that he knew Elson would hear: "Friends, we've just gotten word from the studio about the election of a new baseball commissioner. The club owners have announced that the new commissioner will be our good friend, Leslie O'Connor, long-time aide to the former commissioner Judge Kenesaw Mountain Landis."

Sure enough, Elson picked up the announcement. He repeated it over his station. You can search any list of the commissioners of baseball and you won't find the name of Leslie O'Connor. Brickhouse had duped his old pal, Elson.

Listeners are usually willing to forgive our mistakes, unless those errors reflect a lack of knowledge of baseball. Earl Mann, the Atlanta Cracker executive, once hired an announcer who had the shortest broadcasting stint in the history of Atlanta because he didn't know the game.

This happened in the 1930s when radio wasn't as sophisticated as it is now. Mann was sold a bill of goods by one of the local stations.

"Our announcer," the station told him, "has done big league baseball. He just joined us from Cincinnati where he broadcast the Reds' games. He was well received there and has an outstanding reputation."

"All right," said Earl. "We'll use him."

Came opening day . . . Earl sat in his office, tuned to the broadcast of the new announcer. He noticed a few mistakes along the way.

"Maybe he's nervous. After all, it is his first game," Earl told himself.

The game moved into the ninth inning. The home team (the Crackers) were leading Nashville, 11–3. The Cracker pitcher retired the first hitter, then the second. One out and the game's over.

The announcer said: "There's a fly to left; Cullop has it. That ends the first half of the ninth, Atlanta leading, 11–3. Wait a minute folks, the Crackers are coming off the field. They're bringing their gloves with them. For some reason they're not coming to bat in the last half of the ninth. We'll send over to the press box to find out why."

Before the message got back to the announcer, he had another message from Earl Mann. It said: "You've just broadcast a doubleheader. Your first and your last game!"

7

Jose's Song

BEFORE JOSE FELICIANO AND THE 1968 WORLD SE-ries, the National anthem always had been a routine prelude to sports events.

Robert Merrill, Lucy Monroe, and Gladys Gooding had sung ''The Star-Spangled Banner'' and nobody paid any attention. Then, prior to the fifth World Series game at Detroit on October 7, 1968, Feliciano shook the entire country with his off-beat rendition.

Because I was resident songwriter (as well as the radio voice) of the Tigers, our general manager Jim Campbell asked me to select the singers for the third, fourth, and fifth games to be played at Tiger Stadium.

For the third game (the first at Detroit) my choice was Margaret Whiting. She was female, white, and represented the establishment. Margaret had strong Detroit ties. Her father and uncle, both famous songwriters, were Detroiters, and her sister Barbara still lived there.

For the second game, I picked Marvin Gaye—

male, black, and a top star with a tremendous following. He also lived in Detroit.

The choice for the final Tiger Stadium game was still open when I received a phone call from Mike Gould, a Hollywood publisher.

"Ernie, I heard a young man do a terrific job on 'The Star-Spangled Banner' at the Greek Theater," Mike said. "His name is Jose Feliciano. I think I can get him for you."

"Go ahead," I told him. "The Tigers will not pay him to sing but will pay expenses for him and his group."

At the time, I knew only a few facts about Feliciano. He'd been recording six years and was extremely popular in Latin America. Also, I knew his version of "Light My Fire" was third on the national charts.

To the general public he was unknown; but a month later he was famous.

Jose finished his late show in Las Vegas the morning of October 7 and grabbed the 2:30 a.m. plane to Detroit. I met him when he landed, and he seemed very alert. With him were his wife, Hilda, his seeing-eye dog, Judy, a road manager, and Mike Gould, who had family connections in Jackson, Michigan and also a deep yearning to see the fifth game of the World Series.

During the ride into town, Jose talked baseball. He told me he was a Yankee fan and that he used to hear me broadcast Dodger and Giant games when he was growing up in Harlem. In between baseball talk, he listened to music on the radio and beat out a rhythm on the dashboard of the car.

"I'm so excited," he said. "This is the greatest thing's ever happened to me. Can I meet McLain an

Lolich and Kaline? Can the Tiger's come back? They've got to win today.''

When we reached Tiger Stadium, my first job was to introduce him to the Tigers. I brought in Bill Freehan, Earl Wilson, Al Kaline, Denny McLain, and Mickey Lolich. Jose took his guitar out of the case and began to strum. He improvised lyrics to fit the occasion.

"Come on Kaline, light the fire," he sang. "Tigers got to have desire. Got to win today."

The Tigers loved it.

Time came to go onto the field. Jose, Judy (the dog) and I walked past the packed stands toward center field. The Merle Alvey band was playing, and the Tigers were winding up their fielding practice.

Feliciano began to play his guitar and sing, again improvising. The field mike was open, but the crowd was noisy and I don't think anyone heard his songs and wise-cracks about the Tigers.

Then came the National Anthem. No band accompaniment. Just Jose and his guitar. He stood there on the grass in deep center field, his dog by his side. One small blind Puerto Rican boy and his guitar.

He adjusted his dark glasses. Then he began to strum his guitar and sing.

Since that time, many people have asked me my immediate reaction. Well, when the song was over I knew it had been very different, but I also knew that it was done with great feeling. It had stirred me.

As we walked across the field, Jose asked me, "How did it go?"

"Great!" I told him.

But I heard an angry murmur from the crowd as we

went through the left-field exit. Also, several fans yelled at me and a few at Jose. I couldn't understand their words, but I sensed resentment.

Walking beneath the stands, Jose's road manager asked him, "Didn't you sing it different this time—different than you did at the Greek Theater?"

"Yes, I toned it down," Feliciano told him.

As soon as I took them to their seats, I rushed to my office at Tiger Stadium. The switchboard operator, Tina Faron, told me, "We've been getting hundreds of calls about that singer. People are really mad." In my office was a message to call the press box. It was Hal Middlesworth, Tiger public relations director.

"The AP (Associated Press) man here wants to ask you some questions about Feliciano."

"Okay," I said. "Put him on."

That was the beginning—the start of questions that lasted for two days, steady firing.

After the AP interview, I went to Jose's seat in the grandstand and led the group to their limousine in the parking lot. Jose had seen only two innings, but his plane was scheduled to leave in 45 minutes.

"Have a good trip to Vegas," I told Jose, "and thanks for the job you've done."

"It was a thrill for me," he answered. "I hope I brought the Tigers luck."

He did. The Tigers rallied to beat the Cardinals and keep the Series alive.

That evening in my apartment, the phone was ringing off the hook. Radio men for interviews, newspapermen, TV men—all telling me that a furious reaction was sweeping across the country.

One of the calls was from Ike Pappas of CBS.

"I'd like to bring my TV crew over," he told me, "and film an interview in your apartment for the Walter Cronkite evening report."

It was almost laughable for Cronkite's crew to pick my hotel apartment as a locale. My wife Lulu, who'd flown up from Florida, had been appalled by the severity of my two-room abode. Furniture by Goodwill and Salvation Army. Decor: medium poverty.

"You don't even have a mirror in the bathroom," she reminded me.

"I know. When I shave I see my reflection in the chrome around the medicine cabinet."

Pappas and his CBS crew had trouble fitting into the small room. One cameraman had to stand in the hall and shoot into the apartment, and the sound equipment man also had to work in the hallway.

After the interview, I kept busy answering the phone, expecting some kind of upbraiding from the Tiger brass. But, charitably, no call came from owner John Fetzer or general manager Jim Campbell.

"You're a traitor," one unidentified caller started out. "I bet you were a draft-dodger. You weren't in the service, were you?"

"Four years in the Marines," I told him.

"I don't care," he went on. "Anybody who'd let that long-hair hippie ruin our 'Star-Spangled Banner' has got to be a Communist."

That was when I hung up.

In the morning papers, stories of Jose and the National Anthem almost overshadowed the Tiger victory. Also, there were strong rumors that I might be fired because of the uproar.

Jose was page-one news all over the country. Even

the *New York Times* featured him on the front page. The *Detroit Free Press* front-paged the incident with a two-column photo of Jose singing at Tiger Stadium and this Barbara Stanton lead:

"A blues version of 'The Star-Spangled Banner' hit an unresponsive chord in thousands of World Series fans Monday.

"Outraged fans called Tiger Stadium, the *Free Press*, and local TV stations to complain about the anthem sung by blind Puerto Rican singer Jose Feliciano at the opening of the game."

The follow-up story in the afternoon *Detroit News* ran a page one picture of me and also one of Jose. Richard A. Ryan started his story this way:

"The man who brought Jose Feliciano to Detroit to sing his 'soul' version of 'The Star-Spangled Banner' defended the singer today against critics claiming he mocked the National Anthem.

" 'If anybody's responsible, it's me,' said Ernie Harwell, the Detroit Tiger play-by-play announcer.

"Harwell said it was his suggestion which prompted the Tigers to hire Feliciano—for expenses only—to give his unusual rendition.

". . . 'A lot of people feel it must be sung very formally and staid,' Harwell said after yesterday's game. 'But I think a guy's got a right to put his own feelings into a song.' "

Then Mr. Ryan quoted Jose: "I just do my thing—what I feel—I guess people call it soul, but I don't call it anything.

"I was a little scared when I was asked to sing. I was afraid people would misconstrue it and say I'm making fun of it. But I'm not. It's the way I feel . . .

America is young now and I thought maybe the anthem could be revived now. This country has given me many opportunities. I owe everything to this country. I wanted to contribute something to express my gratitude for what it has done for me. I love this country very much. I'm for everything it stands for. When anyone kicks it, I'm the first to defend it.''

The country seethed over Jose's performance. Editorials lambasted it, civic groups passed angry resolutions. Patients at a Veterans' hospital in Phoenix, Arizona threw shoes at the TV set during the rendition of the song. A TV station in Tampa, Florida announced that if in the future its management didn't approve of the style of a performer's presentation of the National Anthem, the station would cut the sound and insert an approved recording of the song.

Amid the turmoil, Tiger management refrained from criticizing me for selecting Feliciano. However, John Fetzer, Tiger owner and president, wrote me after the Series:

''We have had at least 2,000 complaints on the matter, and the negative position has run a ratio of at least 100–1. I agree with the protestors in that they have the right to say their piece, even though I may not agree with the substance. . . . It is not our purpose to enter into other fields of activity, particularly those involving controversial approaches. . . . This should be well known to you.''

The number of letters addressed directly to me was 305. A total of 185 were against the rendition; 120 wrote in support of it.

Why was the reaction to Jose's singing so intense? Mainly, I think, because the whole country was frus-

trated and needed a definite issue—even a small one—
on which to express a strong opinion.

Riots were still taking place. The war in Vietnam was
a major issue of the day. Drugs and crime-in-the-streets
were causing even more unrest. The campuses were
restless, and the chasm between young and old was
deepening.

Into this vortex stepped Feliciano. The establishment
reacted violently toward him. His wailing, bluesy, rock-
singing style was different. Because he played a guitar
and didn't have a crew-cut, the establishment equated
him with "long-haired hippies." Yet, his hair was not
long. And (as his own statements later proved) his attitudes toward the song and America leaned, if anything, more to the establishment.

Even the dark glasses (worn because of blindness)
prejudiced some against him. All his critics seemed
ready to find something to protest. And they let him
have it—full volley.

At least he awakened interest in "The Star-Spangled
Banner." Now, there is much discussion as to whether
it should be played at sports events. And singers clamor
for a chance to sing the song before the tremendous
audience of a nationally televised game. Andy Williams, Petula Clark, Ethel Ennis, Viki Carr, Lou Rawls,
the Vogues, Jim Nabors, and many others have done
the anthem their own way.

For Feliciano's career, the Detroit incident was a cat-
alyst. The page-one publicity made him a star overnight. Even now when Jose appears on talk shows,
sooner or later his hosts will get around to asking about
his performance at the World Series.

Against Feliciano's wishes, RCA released a single of

his rendition. The record came from Jose's own personal tape. He had taken his tape recorder to center field, attached the mike to the PA mike to tape his moment at the World Series. The record made the charts immediately. In Detroit alone it sold 45,000 within two weeks, despite the fact that none of the major Detroit stations would play the record.

I can still picture that little, blind Puerto Rican in center field of Tiger Stadium, along with his dog and guitar, singing to 55,000 people.

He was a light-hearted, happy kid when he sang the song that afternoon. Happy to be at the World Series; thrilled to be singing his country's National Anthem.

Little did he know that all Hell would soon break loose.

8

Interviews

OFTEN SOMEBODY WILL ASK, "HOW DO YOU SELECT the people you interview on your pre-game show?"

My answer: "I choose the guy who's nearest the tape recorder."

That is a facetious reply, but it has some truth to it.

The most important quality of an interview, I think, is spontaneity. Listeners want to hear a natural conversation between me and a player—or another guest. Too much planning can kill the informality. I never know what questions I'm going to ask. I just start out . . . then I allow the questions to have a natural sequence, determined by the tenor of the answers.

The tape recorder is a modern marvel. It enables all of us who interview to go into the clubhouses, the dugouts, the stands—just about anywhere.

My best interview of 1984 was conducted in the Tiger Stadium weight room—a small room off the clubhouse. Also, that best interview never got on the air.

The Tigers had called up Ruppert Jones from Evansville. He reported to Tiger Stadium a few hours before the night game with the Toronto Blue Jays. I went to the Tiger clubhouse looking for Ruppert. Nobody knew where he was. The press was trying to track him down, too. Accidentally, I wandered into the weight room. Ruppert was there. I was the first to find him.

I did an interview with Jones. He was very open and very expressive. He told how happy he was to be in Detroit. . . . How his faith in God had sustained him after he'd been released by Pittsburgh and had gone to Evansville.

Later I discovered my machine was faulty. The interview was not on the tape. It was too late to do another and I had lost my Ruppert Jones show.

Another interview that didn't get on the air was one I did with Yogi Berra. In those days Yogi and I weren't as close as we are now. He had seen me around the ball park, but didn't always remember my name.

We did the interview in the tunnel between the Yankee dugout and the clubhouse. After each question, Yogi would say, "Yes, Earl," or "That's right, Earl," or "Well, Earl." There was a lot of excess noise in the tunnel and the quality of the tape was poor. After hearing the playback, I decided we should re-do it.

"Yogi," I told him, "we had bad sound on that interview. Those noises in the tunnel ruined it. Would you do the interview again, please? And this time, don't call me Earl, call me Ernie."

"Sure," said Yogi, "I'll do it again, but the real reason is you want me to call you by your right name. Isn't that right?"

Smart man, that Yogi Berra.

One interview, which didn't require a re-take, was one I did with Jack Morris in April 1984. Jack pitched a no-hitter in Chicago. After the game he was ushered to the press box for a mass interview. I was able to grab my tape machine, walk a few steps to the press box and get Jack while he was talking to the group. Then, he stopped by our booth and chatted exclusively with Paul Carey and me.

The most-interviewed Tiger during the championship 1984 season was manager Sparky Anderson. I think his availability to the media reached its regular season zenith when he came back to Anaheim after the death of his father. Sparky had missed several games and everyone in the media wanted to talk with him.

Ordinarily I would have skipped him that night. But I couldn't resist asking his feeling about coming back after the death of his dad. He was gracious, as usual, and talked to me about those feelings.

Not every athlete is as available as Anderson. Once in a while a player will turn you down. I can recall two pitchers who didn't want to be interviewed prior to a game they were to pitch. They were Tommy John and Sam McDowell. Also, I was refused by Mickey Mantle when he was coaching for the Yankees, and once by Rod Carew. But, I can't recall any other turn-downs.

The Mantle refusal was strange. I had interviewed Mickey several times when he was a player. He was never talkative, but he was reservedly pleasant. Then, when he became a broadcaster, he seemed more friendly and often we chatted at length in the press-room. After he had returned to the team as a coach, I approached him in the Yankee clubhouse before a night game.

"How 'bout an interview for my pre-game show?"

"I'd rather not," was his reply.

That was enough of an answer for me. I won't insist. There are plenty of players who are good interviews and ready and willing.

Some interviewers feel you have to bait your subject to get the best answers. I disagree. I feel an interview should be a polite, pleasant conversation, as with a friend. I believe in asking frank questions and not dodging issues.

"If I ask a question you don't want to answer," I tell my subject, "just say so on the interview."

Usually, they go ahead and answer the question anyway.

I had a zany session with Dick (Richie) Allen when he was with the White Sox in 1972. Manager Chuck Tanner played it loose with Allen, so Dick was always reporting to the park an hour or so after the other players.

Allen was having a great year after switching from the National League. He was the Sox's number one star. At Comiskey Park, I waited around for two straight nights, but couldn't keep waiting because time ran out on me. I didn't get to him during that series.

So, I tried again the next week when the Sox came to Detroit. This time I caught him in the clubhouse as he was dressing for the game. It was close to game time.

He agreed to the interview and we started. During the taping he kept looking for a lost sweatshirt.

"I had a sweatshirt, but I can't find it," he said in the middle of the tape. He turned away from the mike while he kept searching through his locker.

"Richie," I asked, "which American League pitchers have been the roughest on you?"

"I don't think you can say any of 'em have been rough," he answered. "But if you'd asked me who the best pitchers in the League are, I could name you several."

"Okay," I said. "Who are the best pitchers in the League?"

His answered floored me.

"I don't think I could name any," he said.

It brought back memories of an interview I had done 30 years before with the University of Georgia football star, Frank Sinkwich.

Frank was a confederate from Youngstown, Ohio, who had brought glory to himself and the Bulldogs. He was the hottest thing in Georgia since cornbread. I took the WSB-Atlanta mobile unit to Athens for a pre-season interview with the South's number one sports headliner.

The previous summer, Sinkwich's weight had been a frenzied topic for the sports pages. Coach Wally Butts had told him he was much too heavy and would have to lose some pounds.

So, my first question: "Frank, last season you weighed 195 and now you're coming into training camp at 178. How do you feel?"

He answered in one word: "Lighter."

You never know what kind of answer you'll get. You never know whether your interviewee will be loose and easy or tight and nervous. Even until you start the interview, you won't know.

One of my biggest surprises was Paul Hornung when I interviewed him on WJBK-TV in Detroit. Paul was the backfield star for the Green Bay Packers at the time.

He came to the studio early (something an interviewer always appreciates). We sat around and chatted easily. He kidded with me and members of the crew.

"This," I told myself, "is going to be a relaxed, fun interview."

I was wrong. As soon as the red light blinked, Hornung froze. The football hero who had performed before packed stadiums in clutch situations was terrified in a quiet studio with only three or four people watching. He just couldn't do it.

In contrast to Hornung was the basketball star, Bill Russell. He was uptight, nervous before we went on. But, as soon as the live interview began, Russell opened up and did an outstanding job for me on our WJBK-TV interview.

While working at WJBK, I ran into one of the strangest mixups in my interviewing career. In 1961 Bobby Hull, of the Chicago Black Hawks, was the fair-haired boy of the hockey world. He was much in demand and very hard to obtain for a show.

"You won't be able to get him to come to the studio," the WJBK program people told me. "He just won't do it."

"I'm going to give a try anyway," I said.

The next morning I got on the phone. I called the Shelby hotel and asked to speak to Mr. Hull. The phone rang in his room.

"Mr. Hull?" I asked.

"Yes."

"I'm Ernie Harwell. I'm doing a five-minute interview show on WJBK-TV tonight at 6:20. I'll pay $35 if you'll come to the studio and go on with me."

"I'll be happy to," was the answer.

I was elated. They had told me I couldn't grab the big guy, but he was coming. At the station, we made all kinds of preparations. The stage hands put a huge photo of Bobby Hull at the back of the set. Promo announcements began to go out over the air that I would be interviewing Hull at 6:20.

About 6 o'clock, my office phone rang. It was the receptionist.

"Ernie," she said, "your guest is here, Mr. Glenn Hall."

"You mean Bobby Hull, don't you?"

"No, Ernie, it's not Bobby Hull. It's Glenn Hall."

Hull and Hall were roommates. My call had reached Glenn Hall. My Southern accent had betrayed me.

All I could do was to explain to Glenn what had happened.

"Don't worry about it," he said. "I'm glad to be here and glad to get the thirty-five bucks. I don't get on too many shows. It's always Bobby they want."

Most baseball managers are easy interviews. One exception: Billy Martin. Billy is a good talker, but he is uneven. You'll ask him a question and he's likely to give you a very short answer. Or, when you have to cut the show short, he might keep talking on and on. He's always been a pal of mine, but it seems sometimes that he's trying to bedevil you during an interview. I've had other radio-TV men tell me they have the same reaction to Martin.

One of my favorite managers to interview was Eddie Stanky. He and I went back a long way. We were very close when I broadcast for the Giants in the early Fifties and he was their scrappy second baseman. Whenever we were together we were always throwing verbal harpoons at each other. Yet, he was one of my best friends.

I did a tape with him in spring training. It was Eddie's first month as White Sox manager.

"Ed," I asked, "you're coming over to Chicago from managing the Cardinals. Will you use the same managerial methods you used with the Cards, or will you change?"

"Ernie," he shot back, "I used to listen to you when you broadcast in Baltimore. Are you still broadcasting that way? I hope not. No wonder they fired you."

Later in the season, Stanky came into Tiger Stadium with the White Sox. It was interview time again. Before I could even ask a question, he jumped in.

"Ernie, I know about you," he said. "I know you picked us to finish sixth. You're gonna be wrong again, Ernie. And, by the way, how is Lulu? I've eaten at your house. Is she still trying to poison everybody?"

Does that sound like a real pal, or not?

Anyway, that is Eddie Stanky.

Baseball's easiest interview had to be Casey Stengel. Some of his answers are legends in themselves. The last interview I did with Casey was in 1972 at the American League playoffs. He had been out of baseball for five years, but he was still hot copy. It was a five-minute interview. All I did was ask one question and Casey was off and running. The irony of the interview was that Casey didn't even want to go on the air. I found him in the VIP room at Oakland Stadium and asked if I might have an interview.

"Don't think I want to talk on no interview," he told me. "I just want to wait here for Mrs. Stengel."

I sat down. He began to talk with me—off the air.

After eight or ten minutes he turned to me and said, "I'll go on the air with you. Why don't we do that radio thing right now?" And we did.

Casey was the first person George Kell ever interviewed in his radio-TV career.

George had retired from the Orioles after the 1957 season. He was hired by CBS-TV to do an interview show before each "Game of the Week" telecast. He phoned me in Baltimore.

"I'm doing this show," he said. "My first guest will be Casey Stengel. Give me some ideas about what to ask him."

"Might be good, George," I told him, "to talk to Casey about how he makes up his batting order. That is, what qualities he looks for in a leadoff man, a No. 2 hitter, and on down the line."

Next time I saw George I asked him how it went.

"Great," he said. "But, in the 15 minutes, Casey didn't get past the leadoff hitter."

Another non-stop talker was Frank (Trader) Lane, the GM of many big league clubs. Once when I got through interviewing Frank, I told him, "Putting you on a five-minute tape is like inscribing the New Testament on a grain of rice."

One of the finest gentlemen I ever met in sports was the late Bobby Jones. He was still playing in the Masters tournament when I covered that event in Augusta, Georgia in the early 1940s. Portable equipment was unknown in those days. To conduct an interview, I would ask the principals to leave the comfort of the clubhouse and come to a tower near the 18th green.

Bob Jones (even then suffering with chronic back pain) did just that. He walked through the rain and chill of an Augusta spring, climbed the tower and talked with me for 15 minutes. He was interesting and entertaining as he discussed everything about golf except himself and his own game.

Another Georgian in the sports limelight during my early days of radio was Rudy York. Rudy—unlike the gentle Mr. Jones—pulled the big-time act on me.

I had started at WSB in the spring of 1940 with a twice-a-night 15-minute sports show. That was the season York starred for the Detroit Tigers in the World Series.

After the Series, the city of Cartersville, Georgia gave a testimonial banquet for York. I was invited to be the emcee. So, I figured this would be a good time to interview the hitting star of the World Series.

Engineer Mark Tolson and I left the station in the WSB truck, carrying the heavy, so-called portable equipment. We were about halfway on the 80-mile journey when Tolson discovered he had left the microphones at the station. We returned, picked up the mikes and were on our way again.

Still, we reached the banquet hall early. York was there, too. I told him I would like to interview him before dinner.

"Sorry, I can't do that," he said. "I have an agent now. Had one since the Series. I don't do any interviews until he sets the fee."

That was the end of that—no interview. Believe me, I felt strange that night as the emcee, paying tribute to the local boy who made good—the same one who had turned down my interview request.

Also, it was my first encounter with a player who had

an agent. In 1940 he was one of a kind. Today, even the ".210 hitters have agents.

There was no agent, but an agency, involved in an interview with Fred Miller, the head man of Miller Brewing Co. I was broadcasting the New York Giants football games with Marty Glickman. The Giants were to play the Green Bay Packers at Milwaukee, and the advertising agency for Miller Brewing asked me to interview Fred Miller at half-time.

Miller was a former player and had been an assistant football coach. He knew the game and he was articulate. But the agency was taking no chances, with Miller or with me. They provided a written script for the interview—questions by me and answers from Fred Miller. It was the only time in my career I had interviewed with a script.

Celebrities are the toughest interviews during the sports events. Usually they show up in the booth during the play-by-play. The difficulty comes in working them in over the play-by-play description of the game.

Milton Berle was one of the best at adapting to this difficulty. He knew baseball and realized the demands of the play-by-play. Vice President Bush was another who sized up the situation. I interviewed him during the 1984 World Series.

After a couple of questions, the Vice President said, "Ernie, you better quit talking with me and get back to the game."

In a round-about way, one of my most successful interviews during a game was one with Homer and Jethro, the RCA recording artists. A dee-jay friend of mine, George Toles, had arranged for them to see a game from my booth. After the game, Jethro said to me,

"That was fun, Ernie. Homer and I are going to use one of your songs on our next album."

That fall my song, "Upside Down," appeared on their RCA album, and the album notes referred to their visit to the Tiger game.

9

And They Called It The Birth of The Boos

ONE NIGHT IN CLEVELAND, I MADE A VISIT TO THE umpires' room in Municipal Stadium. Umpire Jim Evans said, "Ernie, you've talked on the radio about us rubbing up the baseballs before the game. Why don't you do the rubbing for us tonight?"

Jim showed me how to dip my hand into a tin can of Delaware River mud, spread the mud over the baseball and rub.

Nobody but Jim Evans and his crew knew that I prepared the balls for the Tiger-Cleveland game that night. But that was a real treat for me because umpires always have been special to me throughout my career.

In my Southern League days, I knew some of the real old-timers. The most interesting and colorful was Harry (Steamboat) Johnson. Back in 1914 Steamboat had a short stint in the National League, but always claimed he didn't make it because the ever-powerful John McGraw didn't like him.

Johnson umpired for 35 years. He wrote a book that wasn't a best-seller but it was a near-miss. One afternoon in Chattanooga he called a batter out and heard something whir past his ear. It was not a familiar sound to Steamboat—like that of a pop bottle. Then, plop. Right at home plate landed a copy of Johnson's own book, *Standing the Gaff.*

When I worked in the National League, Babe Pinelli, Bill Stewart, Larry Goetz, and Jocko Conlon were special friends of mine.

Goetz was a great example to me that umpires work under the same kind of pressure as the players. One of the most exciting games in World Series history was the fourth game of the 1947 Series at Ebbets Field. Cookie Lavagetto of the Dodgers drove in the tying and winning runs with the only hit of the game off the Yankee pitcher, Floyd Bevens.

The game was over. The Dodger fans were going crazy.

After the field had emptied, umpire Goetz was still at home plate. He grabbed his whiskbroom and furiously began to dust off the plate—for the start of the next World Series game.

I broadcast a Dodger game in old Braves Field in Boston and saw George Barr eject a player for wearing a raincoat. This was the second game of a doubleheader on September 29—a cold, dark and rainy afternoon. The Dodgers had won the opener, 9–2.

Rain and darkness made Don Newcombe's fastball even more menacing. The Brave hitters were reluctant to come to the plate. They began to stall. The Dodgers had an eight-run lead, but the umpires weren't giving in. As early as the third inning, they had decided to get this one through at least five innings.

Tommy Holmes led off the fifth for the Braves. As he came to bat, the plate umpire George Barr took a glance toward the on-deck circle. Kneeling there was Connie Ryan, the Braves infielder. Connie was wearing a raincoat. Except for his Braves' baseball cap, he could have been a New England fisherman fighting a squall.

When Barr saw the raincoat, his thumb went into the air. "Get outta the game, Ryan," he screamed. I never found out if Connie wore his raincoat when he took his shower a few minutes later.

Jocko Conlon was another National League umpire who had a lot of spunk. Jocko was a White Sox outfielder when he became an umpire by accident. He was pressed into service in a 1935 game when umpire Red Ormsby was overcome by the heat. He liked that small taste of umpiring and decided to make it his profession. He made the Hall of Fame at Cooperstown because he had a great talent, a keen pride in his profession, and a special flair for running a game.

When he was in charge, Jocko did not like whining players. In one particular game Richie Ashburn, the Phillie outfielder, moaned about one pitch too many.

"All right, Ashburn," Jocko told him. "You umpire. I'm letting you call the next pitch."

"You're kidding," said Ashburn.

"I am not. You call the next one."

The next pitch was a foot outside. Ashburn took a look at it and said, "Strike."

Conlon put his right arm up to signal the strike. Then he called time. He went out to dust off the plate. Jocko looked up at Ashburn and said, "Richie, I gave you the only chance a hitter ever had in the history of baseball to bat and umpire at the same time. You blew it. That's the last pitch you'll ever call. I'm not gonna have you louse up my profession.''

When I first came to the American League in 1954, the umpire I knew the best was Ed Rommel. He lived in Baltimore while I was broadcasting the Oriole games and I used to see a lot of Ed and his wife Em in the off-season. I asked him once why anybody would want to be an umpire.

''I became one,'' he answered, ''because it was the only way I could stay in baseball.''

Umpires have the toughest job in baseball. Ever since the birth of the boos, they have suffered more abuse than a washroom wall. A major league umpire must have good eyesight, good disposition, good health, complete knowledge of the rules, and the respect of his co-workers. Handling the ballplayers calls for varied treatments. Some must be left alone, others pushed a little, and others patted on the back.

To me, a good umpire is like a good driver. If he is doing his job properly, you seldom notice him.

I think the modern-day umpire is much superior to the ones I knew in the 1940s and 1950s. The leagues make them retire earlier now. We get a better-conditioned and harder-working group of men. Yet, the umpires of today are sometimes too willing to keep an argument going. In earlier days, the highly qualified umpires walked away from arguments. These days you can even see some of the umps bait the players into extending their confrontations.

Ed Hurley was one of the worst in this respect. When he umpired in the American League, he would practically follow a player into the dugout to keep an argument alive.

Today's umpires are better paid and better educated. In the American League now many of them have responsible off-season occupations. Joe Brinkman heads up an umpiring school. Bill Kunkel, who fought back bravely and beat cancer, volunteers his services for the American Cancer Society. Durwood Merrill has his own radio show. Nick Bremigan writes a syndicated column on baseball rules. And—how's this for a fancy title— Rocky Roe is a member of the Board of Directors of the Computer Method Corporation. Those are just a few of the examples of the savvy and versatility of the modern umpire.

The one quality all of them have—the new and the old—is an ardent devotion to baseball. Contrary to public opinion, the umpires are not lonely men. They have more friends than the players in the cities they visit. I always enjoy my visit to the umps' dressing rooms. They are great kidders. They are open and friendly. I've found all of them willing to discuss the interpretation of the rules and any other phase of their profession.

The umpires don't last as long as they once did. Bill Klem umpired for 36 seasons. Tommy Connolly worked for 34. After the 1984 season, the senior American League umpire Marty Springstead had put in 19 years. The longevity record among the current National League umpires belongs to Doug Harvey who completed his 23rd year in 1984.

Whether an ump is in his first year or his 23rd, you can bet he'll be singled out as a target for abuse from the players. There are no secrets in baseball and the players can zero in when they find a weak spot in an umpire's background.

There was an umpire many years ago named Charlie

Moran who was vulnerable in two areas. He coached the Praying Colonels football team at Centre College and he raised bird dogs. Once when Moran called Fresco Thompson out on a pitch which almost beheaded Fresco, Thompson turned and yelled: "Now I know why they called Centre the Praying Colonels. If you coached them like you umpire, they had to pray to win a game."

Moran once sold a bird dog to Hughie Critz, a weak-hitting Giant infielder, while Critz was batting against the Chicago Cubs.

"They tell me you got some good dogs," Critz said to the umpire. "What are you asking for a good one?"

The pitcher wound up and threw.

"A hundred and fifty dollars," Moran replied. "Ball one."

"That's a lot of money," said Critz.

"Best dog in America. Strike one."

"Is he fast?"

"Fast? He can outrun a train. Ball two."

"What color?"

"Liver and white. Real handsome animal. Strike two."

"Can he retrieve?"

"Through hell and high water. Ball three."

"Okay. I'll take him."

"That's fine. Ball four. Take your base."

Gabby Hartnett, the Cubs' catcher, whipped off his mask, wheeled around, and stuck his reddening face toward the Umpire Moran.

"If it's all the same to you, Charlie," he raged, "don't be selling any more bird dogs to .200 hitters while they're up here at the plate."

The relationship between player and ump has always been a vital part of baseball. But the relationship between manager and umpire is even more crucial. Here we see the duel of the two authority figures in the game. Actually, the game belongs to the umpire. He should be in command. Yet, he realizes that each manager commands his own team and the manager cannot afford to lose face with his players. So, there is a constant tug-of-war between the manager and the umpire.

It was ironic that Ty Cobb, the most competitive man in baseball history, played it cool with umpires. "Never bait an umpire," Cobb used to say. "If you have a legitimate beef, go ahead and speak your piece. But don't try to intimidate them."

Earl Weaver, Billy Martin, and Paul Richards came from the other school. Umpire Ed Rommel told me that Richards was the most masterful at verbally excoriating the umps. "He insulted with words that even I had never heard."

Earl Weaver was a tough one, too. The umpires despised Weaver more than any other manager. Weaver had a trick with his cap. He pressed its visor into a point, then jabbed it into the umpire's face.

The umpires never cared for Billy Martin, either. Billy was a screamer and a dirt-kicker. Strangely enough, Martin sometimes could conduct a very calm and cogent argument.

Connie Mack probably was the calmest of all in the manager-ump relationship. His stature as the patriarch of baseball commanded that the umpires come over to the dugout and talk with him if Mr. Mack thought such a discussion was needed.

Jimmy Dykes, who played many years for Mack, was smart and sly. Most of the time Jimmy was laid back, but he could get sarcastic and cutting. Also, Jimmy had his small tricks. His 22 years as a player and 21 as a manager had taught him a few.

As a manager, Jimmy would write out his batting order card in very light pencil and deliver it to the umpires during the home plate conference. Then the ump would say: "Hey Jimmy, this is so faint, I can hardly read it."

Dykes would answer: "Now you should know why I've been complaining about your eyesight all these years."

The umpires' social life revolves around their friends in various cities. Sometimes it's golf and sometimes just a quiet lunch or dinner. In St. Louis one friend went even further. For years Arthur Donnelly, a funeral director, provided free transportation for the umpires— limousine service to and from the ball park. One afternoon at old Sportsman Park, Mr. Donnelly had seen umpire Frank (Silk) O'Loughlin attacked by fans. He felt that Silk and his fellow umpires needed protection. Before he died, Donnelly decreed in his will that his survivors always provide transportation for the umpires whenever they were in St. Louis.

The funeral home no longer exists and the umpires now take care of their own transportation, but it was a custom they appreciated while it lasted.

Umpires will tell you they have to be thick-skinned to survive. Yet, I have never seen one who is not sensitive about his eyesight. Steamboat Johnson carried a card attesting to his 20–20 vision. He would whip out that card whenever anybody questioned his eyesight. Only a few umpires dared to wear glasses. Ed Rommel and Frank Umont of the American League are the only ones I can recall. Before the 1984 season started, the

American League retired Russ Goetz because his eyesight did not measure up and he refused to wear glasses.

The umpire is a vital part of baseball. He protects the game at a crucial spot—the playing field. It's symbolic that the game does not begin until the umpire says, "Play ball," and it doesn't end until he declares the final out. (Actually, most umpires say that they do not cry out, "Play ball," at the start of a game. That's for the movies or TV shows. Most of them say, "Let's go," or some such phrase.)

The starting salary for a major league umpire is $30,000 and he can make as much as $80,000 per year, depending on his years of service. Umpiring is a job unto itself—unlike most any other. It might be best summed up by the dialogue between famous old arbiters—Silk O'Loughlin and Tim Hurst. O'Loughlin was bemoaning his fate as an umpire.

"What a life," he said to Hurst. "You can't call it a dog's life because most people like dogs. Even a criminal on trial is considered innocent until they convict him. But look at us. Lower than the scum of the earth, worthy of no man's praise and every man's scorn. Any pop-off with the price of a bleacher ticket feels it's his privilege to shower us with abuse in our job and . . ."

"Sure, Silk," interrupted Hurst, "but you can't beat them hours!"

10

A Deeper Dedication

I T'S NOT OFTEN THAT BIG LEAGUERS HAVE A CHANCE to socialize with opposing players. Fraternization on the field is forbidden. Before each game the umpires sit in the stands and report such infractions.

So, generally, socializing is reduced to a brief word around the batting cage or a casual meeting outside the park.

In mid-season 1984, three Baltimore Orioles overcame this barrier by visiting a Tiger Bible study at Tiger Stadium. It was the most heart-warming experience for me in that exciting '84 Tiger year.

To supplement the Baseball Chapel, my son Gray was conducting a Bible study with the Tigers once a week when the Tigers were at home. I asked Scotty McGregor, Wayne Gross, and Storm Davis of the Orioles to join us.

They came over to the weight room—just outside the Tigers' clubhouse—for our meeting on Tuesday, September 4. After a short talk, Gray called on the members of the Tigers and the Orioles for comments.

Scotty spoke first: "I'm blessed to be here with you guys," he said. "But you Tigers seem to me to be tense. I don't think you're really enjoying yourselves. You've got a big lead. Looks like nobody's going to catch you. Last year when we won the pennant and the World Series, we had fun. I'm impressed by the type of people on your team. And I know that if you win, many of you will give the glory to God and not take the credit for yourselves."

"I've got to agree with Scotty," Storm Davis added. "The biggest thrill I got last year in winning the championship was the fact that we were able to let people know our talents came from the Lord and without Him we would have been nothing."

"There are some teams," said McGregor, "that I wouldn't even want to play for. But our team had the right attitude and I think the Tigers do, too. I'd like to see you guys relax a little. Enjoy the rest of the season."

The Tigers were impressed. Ruppert Jones, Howard Johnson, and the others took those words to heart.

"I appreciate your saying that, Scotty," John Grubb told the Baltimore pitcher. "I've wanted to speak up but sometimes it's hard for me. I needed that encouragement."

"You've got to remember," McGregor added, "that baseball's not the most important part of our lives. It's what we do for God. We are what we are because of Him."

"I found that out this season in the minors," said Ruppert Jones. "I was feeling low when I couldn't get a big league job. But I went to Evansville and I had a feeling that the Lord would take care of me. And he has.''

''That's important, Ruppert,'' said McGregor. ''Last year when I pitched the first game of the World Series against the Phils, I was nervous. I had a 1–0 lead, but somehow never felt right. I lost that lead and the game. Then, I came back in the fifth game. This time, I told the Lord the game was His. I was going to relax and enjoy it. I shut 'em out, 5–0, and we took the title. That's what I mean when I say you guys have got to relax.''

You could tell the Tigers were touched. I looked around the room. Most of these big clunks had tears in their eyes. They had heard God's word from a fellow athlete who had been where they were headed, and who had won the World Series clincher.

The Tigers lost that night to Baltimore and the next night, too. After that they went to Toronto and swept a three-game weekend series, knocking the Blue Jays out of the race. A week later in Detroit, they beat Milwaukee to assure themselves of the Eastern Division title.

As they went on to sweep Kansas City in the playoffs and win the World Series, some of those Tigers had a chance to express their religious convictions and to credit God for their victories.

Such testimonies were unheard of in earlier baseball days. But now, mainly because of the strength of Baseball Chapel, many major league stars have made their religious beliefs public. Lance Parrish, Gary Carter, Davey Johnson, Bob Boone, George Foster, Mike Schmidt, Andre Thornton, Dan Quisenberry, and Robin Yount are just a few.

Baseball Chapel has its roots in the early informal meetings of players for the Minnesota Twins and the Chicago Cubs. Led by Jim Kaat and Alan Worthington, the Twins began to meet Sunday mornings at their hotel. Meanwhile, the Cubs were doing the same thing under the guidance of Randy Hundley and Don Kessinger. The teams would have doughnuts and coffee, do some praying, and listen to a speaker.

A few years later, the Tigers and other teams began to meet. Behind the Tiger meetings was Watson Spoelstra. Waddy had been a hard-drinking, fast-living sportswriter for the *Detroit News*. When his daughter lingered near death, he dedicated his life to Jesus with the promise that he would serve the Lord in any way He directed.

"That direction," Waddy said later, "was to organize the Baseball Chapel and take the Gospel to the major league players."

I remember those early meetings. Sometimes Waddy and I and one or two Tigers would make up the entire audience. It was often embarrassing that a speaker would take the time and effort to come in all the way from the suburbs to speak to such a small group.

In the mid-60s the group began to grow. Dave Wickersham and Don Demeter came to the Tigers and brought added strength to the group. Progress was still slow.

In 1973 Spoelstra officially organized the Baseball Chapel. The ministry spread to all clubs in the major leagues. Waddy flew to New York and laid out the plans for his program before the baseball commissioner, Bowie Kuhn.

"It was his encouragement and support that helped us get started," Waddy says.

The clubs kept on meeting on Sundays in the hotels. But it was a harried, frantic time.

"Why don't we move the meetings to the ball parks," I suggested to Waddy. "At the hotel, everybody's in a hurry on Sunday. It's usually get-away day and that means eating breakfast, packing, checking out, and catching the team bus. Also, sometimes it's hard to get a room to meet in at the hotel."

"Let's give it a try," Waddy agreed.

We did and it worked. The players seemed more relaxed in their own environment. It was easier for the speakers to get to the ball park and it also meant the speakers could stay and enjoy the game. Now, all the teams—except one—meet at the park. The only exception is the Texas Rangers. Manager Doug Rader prefers his guys to meet at the hotel.

A typical Sunday at Tiger Stadium now would find the speaker (sometimes a pastor, sometimes a layman) coming first to the visiting clubhouse. The visitors hold their chapel at 11:30 a.m. After speaking to the visitors for 15 or 20 minutes, the speaker will take a break and head for the Tiger clubhouse. The Tigers will meet with him at 12:15.

The visitors' clubhouse is quite cramped, so everybody grabs a metal stool and gathers in the shower room to hear the speaker.

The standard joke is: "If the speaker gets too fiery, we can always turn on the showers."

Players from both clubs are strictly informal. Most of them come in underwear or partially in uniform. They sit on tables, stools, or even the floor. Each team has a chapel leader who will introduce the speaker.

I've spoken to several teams. In addition to the Tigers, I have spoken to the Royals, Blue Jays, Red Sox, Yankees, and (in spring training) the Cardinals, Phillies, and Mets. Also, I've talked to several minor league and instructional league teams. The players always are most attentive to the speakers. And, when the program is over, they file by to shake the speaker's hand and give him a comment. During these sessions I have seen many young men dedicate their lives to Christ.

From the chapel services have come the development of weekly Bible studies for many clubs. With some teams, the players' wives become involved. One season when many of the Tiger families lived on the Northwest side of Detroit, the players and their wives came to our home every Thursday for Bible study. They brought their kids and we served coffee, juice, and doughnuts.

To me these sessions with the whole families were even more rewarding than the ones with only the players. The wives participated in the discussions and their Christian support was a strength for their husbands.

The Chapel program has spread to the minor leagues. Now 140 minor league teams have services. And similar chapels are conducted in pro football, basketball, golf, and bowling.

Why do major league players who have so much fame and money turn to Christ? I think it's because once they reach their boyhood goals, they discover there is still a deep emptiness in their lives.

"I had always considered myself a Christian," Bob Boone says, "but not until I attended Bible study and chapel did I realize there were voids in my life and I had a deep need for Christ.''

Drugs, alcohol, and sex are great temptations to baseball players. They are young and virile. They live in a physical environment. They are away from home at least half the time. Adulation has followed them since high school days. Chapel helps with its answers. But, an even more powerful influence on a teammate is the example of a truly committed Christian, living the Christian life.

''They can doubt what you say, but they have to believe what you do'' is one of my favorite sayings.

Remember the Fritz Peterson-Mike Kekich case? It shook the baseball world in 1973. The two were pitchers with the Yankees that year and close friends. They decided to swap wives. You can imagine how the Yankee brass and all of baseball reacted. But the two pals went through with their plan. Both were traded away from the Yankees. Both were out of baseball within four years.

Kekich drifted away. He went to Mexico to get a medical degree and now is a resident physician at an Albuquerque hospital. Meanwhile, Fritz Peterson was searching to find himself. Even as a Yankee, he had read many self-help books trying to locate his niche. From the Yankees, he had gone to the Cleveland team and then to the Texas Rangers. In his final year in baseball, 1976, he became a teammate of Danny Thompson, who that year played 64 games for the Rangers.

Danny Thompson was dying of leukemia. He knew it and all his teammates knew it. But the way he lived had a profound effect on Fritz Peterson.

''When I saw Danny Thompson at Texas,'' Fritz recalls, "I saw something I'd been looking for. I didn't know at the time what it was, but I knew it was what I had needed."

Fritz talked with Thompson.

"Danny," he told him, "tell me what makes you so different. How can I be like you?"

Thompson told Peterson that he credited everything in his life to his religious faith. Fritz, that year in Texas, dedicated his life to Jesus. Danny Thompson died after the '76 season. But Fritz Peterson is now a frequent chapel speaker and his message has deeply touched the lives of many big league players.

11

It's More Than Merely Muscle

ALL OF US LIVE WITH PRESSURE.

The housewife has to drive the kids to school in heavy traffic. The husband fends off an angry boss at the office. To the major league ballplayer, pressure can be a time at bat in a crucial spot, or a grounder hit to him in a double-play situation.

In the stretch days of the 1984 season, Tiger manager Sparky Anderson looked down the bench for his pinch-hitter. He knew the man he wanted for that particular spot.

"But when I saw the guy's face, I knew I couldn't use him," he recalled. "His face was white. He was scared even before I was ready to call on him."

Anderson settled for another hitter and bypassed his first selection several times during the rest of the season.

Eddie Stanky used to say there was no such thing as pressure.

"It's just something invented by the media," he told

me. "I go out and play every game. It's my day-to-day job. Pressure is something to read about in the papers and hear about over the air."

That's easy for him to say. He was a clutch pitcher. The kind any manager dreams about for his team. But not all players are Eddie Stankys.

One of our Baseball Chapel speakers had a good explanation of pressure.

"Put a plank on the ground. It's easy to walk on," he said. "But put that same plank 35 stories above the ground between two buildings, and the walk on it from one building to another is no simple matter. That is pressure."

Some players thrive on pressure. Kirk Gibson of the Tigers is one. In the final game of the 1984 Series, he responded to pressure with a three-run homer in the eighth inning to beat the Padres.

"I want to be at the plate in a tough situation," he explained. "I love to be at bat when the game is on the line. It brings out the best in me."

Two young Tiger pitchers showed a positive response to pressure the last days of '84. Roger Mason won his first major league victory by beating Milwaukee, 7–3, to clinch a tie for the division championship. The next night rookie Randy O'Neal won the division clincher for the Tigers in his first major league start. He beat Milwaukee, 3–0.

O'Neal threw four straight forkballs to the Brewer slugger Cecil Cooper on a 3–2 count. Cooper looked at the rookie with one of those "You're not supposed to do that" glares. After that, O'Neal knew he belonged.

Yet, there are many rookies—and even veterans—who can't withstand pressure. They drift back home and sell insurance to their old high school classmates.

Pressure creates fear. And fear has driven almost as many prospects from the big leagues as the curve.

Players don't want to talk about fear. But it hides inside many of them. There is a fear of being hit by a pitch, a fear of making an error in a crucial moment and, strangely enough, even the fear of success.

Several years ago a successful major league catcher had to fight fear whenever he came to bat. He made himself a good hitter; but still he had that feeling of fear. It even affected him on defense. His manager ordered the catcher to signal to his pitcher for a brush-back pitch.

"Skip," he told the manager, "I don't like to do that. That other pitcher knows where a brush-back sign is coming from. He'll retaliate when I come to bat."

Careers have been ruined by the fear of being hit. Many minor-leaguers don't make it to the majors because they can't subdue their fear. Some major-leaguers lose their skills after bean-ball incidents.

Gates Brown, for years a Tiger batting coach, told me that the Detroit third baseman Don Wert was never the same hitter after he had been beaned.

Others can conquer the fear.

"Best I ever saw at that," Gates says, "was Willie Horton. He got hit one time on the bill of his batting helmet. His eye was swollen shut. He came back and crowded the plate even more."

Gates himself got a bean-ball baptism his very first year with the Tigers—1964.

"It was the scaredest I've ever been," he says. "Pedro Ramos was pitching against us in Cleveland. Al Kaline hit two shots off him. I stepped into the box after Kaline's second hit. Ramos isn't even looking at the plate and cuts one loose—right at my head. It was the only time I'd ever heard an umpire yell, 'Look out.' "

I asked the fine Yankee hitter Dave Winfield about fear at the plate. He said: "I don't think it's fear. With me, it's an uncertainty. When I fail, that uncertainty builds within me. I have to be aggressive and have no fear of being hit. I cannot let the pitcher intimidate me. Some like to pitch me inside. If I think it's intentional, I'll go out to the mound after the pitcher."

Winfield points to Don Baylor as a hitter who can't be intimidated. "Look at him," says Dave. "Right on top of the plate. They pitch him tight, he gets hit a lot, but he never gives an inch."

Sparky Anderson says the best at not being intimidated at the plate are Lee May, Pete Rose, and Chet Lemon.

"There are some players today," says Sparky, "who couldn't stand up to the rough, knock-'em-down pitching of thirty years ago. But these three could handle themselves in any baseball era. None of them has any fear at the plate."

One of the strangest fears to beset a baseball player is the catcher's fear of throwing the ball back to the pitcher. This is not even a pivotal play in a game. Most of the time a bad throw to the pitcher would be harmless. But it is most embarrassing.

Mike Ivie had this fear and couldn't conquer it. He moved to first base, and still had a problem with delivering the ball to the pitcher. Ivie could stand at the plate and let a 90-mile-an-hour fastball whiz toward him, but he couldn't get over his fear of a poor throw.

"Ivie might have been the best natural player I ever saw," Roger Craig told me. "When I managed him at San Diego, I thought his potential was limitless. He could hit with power, he was a good fielder and he could throw. But something happened to him to give him a mental block. I think I spent more time with Ivie than any other player I was ever associated with. I liked him and he liked me but somehow he never made it.''

Clint Courtney was another who was haunted by the catcher-to-the-pitcher toss. Courtney was a tough, roughneck battler who never gave up. When catching for the St. Louis Browns he took on the entire Yankee team almost single-handedly. He had spirit and determination and, except for the quirk of throwing to the pitcher, he was fearless. Certainly, he was the last player you'd think of as a candidate for such a weakness.

Clint would almost walk the ball back to the pitcher. He realized his weakness and worked on it in morning practice sessions. And was able to overcome it somewhat. But somehow it always came back to haunt him.

Ray Fosse, John Edwards, and Dave Engel are other catchers who have faced the same types of fear that bothered Ivie and Courtney. Fear seems to afflict catcher and pitcher more than any other position.

Fear's most celebrated victim among pitchers was Steve Blass, the Pittsburgh right-hander who was a World Series hero in 1971 and then disappeared from the baseball world before the next Series came around.

Coach after coach worked with Blass. He simply couldn't get his pitches over the plate. A mental block had scrambled whatever control device had made him an outstanding pitcher and World Series hero.

A symbolic climax in the Blass story came when he appeared at an Old-Timers' game several years after his retirement. He was brought in to pitch and still could not locate the plate.

"I can't pitch for a contender. Trade me to a non-contending team." That was the self-analytical demand of Dick (Turk) Farrell, the hard-living, tough-talking Philadelphia Phillie pitcher. Those who knew Farrell would never have pictured him as the type to confess to such a shortcoming.

Managers and pitching coaches have often wondered about their pitchers: "Is the arm really sore? Or, is it in the head?" Not even a psychiatrist can answer that question. Many pitching careers have ended with a twinge in the shoulder or elbow. Some of the hurts have been physical; many of them are psychological.

Remember Mark (the Bird) Fidrych? He blazed across the baseball skies when he pitched for a mediocre Detroit team in 1976. He talked to the baseball, won 19 victories, and captured the hearts of the whole nation.

After that one year, Mark hurt his arm and was never the same. For several seasons he tried to come back. During one of his efforts I interviewed him in the Tiger clubhouse at Kansas City.

"Mark, you're back on the active list now. How is the arm feeling?" I asked.

"Oh, it's feeling real good, Ernie."

"What does the Tiger team doctor, Dr. Clarence Livingood, say about your arm?"

"Oh, Dr. Livingood. He don't know about arms. He's a skin doctor. One of them gynecologists."

Fidrych continued to struggle with his arm problems. Then he seemed to be ready physically. However, even with his arm back in shape he was never able to regain the ability he showed in that one brilliant season.

Many in the Tiger organization felt that the Bird's

comeback was deterred as much by a mental block as by any kind of arm ailment.

"He seemed to be completely confused," one of his coaches said. "He threw as well as he did before. But it just couldn't happen for him again."

Another enthusiastic, crowd-pleasing Tiger pitcher of recent years, Kevin Saucier, met an even quicker demise than Fidrych. "Hot Sauce," as the fans named him, was joyous and effervescent after his victorious relief stints in 1981, his first Tiger season. Over one span, he relieved 20 times and allowed only one run in 31⅔ innings. During that streak, he notched one victory and ten saves and posted an ERA of 0.28.

Then the next year he lost it. The plate began to move around on "Hot Sauce." His pitches sailed to the backstop. He fought himself. He tried different deliveries. He listened to numerous theories.

Nothing worked. The Tigers gave up on Saucier and sent him to Evansville. He won none and lost four. He never regained his control. He quit baseball and headed home to Pensacola to run a tavern and play softball.

There are many like him. Many who would handle the pressure for a time but then one day no longer could. They're playing softball somewhere and telling the guys at the tavern how they used to pitch to George Brett or Stan Musial, or Hank Aaron or Babe Ruth.

12

"Report Me and My Cause Aright"

Shakespeare, *Hamlet*
Act IV, Scene 2

DETROIT TIGER PITCHER JACK MORRIS QUIT TALKING in the middle of the 1984 season.

When Morris had pitched his no-hitter at Chicago in April, he was the darling of the media. But now, his world had turned sour. He was losing. His arm was hurting and he didn't want to talk.

"Lock-jaw set in" was the way one of the Detroit writers put it.

Jack thought the media had mistreated him. Now that he was losing, the writers were writing unkind words about him.

"They've invaded my privacy. I have no time to myself or my family," he said. "From now on, I'm not talking. From now on, I know I won't be misquoted."

Morris remained silent until the final months of the season. Manager Sparky Anderson talked him out of his sulk. And by the time the Tigers clinched the pennant, Morris was once again in communication with the media.

He was another example of the widening gulf between the player and the media. Each year that gulf becomes more evident. The friction is greater between player and writer than it is between the player and radio and TV. Players put more trust in microphones than in pad and pencil.

"At least I know I can't be misquoted in a TV interview," a veteran star told me. "But, in the paper, there can be a lot of twisting around. And a headline can be damaging sometimes even when the actual story isn't."

Even Alan Trammell, one of the most approachable of the Tigers, turned his back on the writers in midseason 1984. But he quickly came back to his senses.

Why this distrust? Why are the players turning away from the writers?

Money is one reason. The players make so much money that they feel they don't need the writers. The distrust has always been there. Now the million-dollar contracts have accentuated it.

In the Thirties, Giant manager Bill Terry was referring to those who covered his club as "$35-a-week reporters." Thirty-five dollars won't buy a decent dinner in most New York restaurants now, but the gulf between athlete and writer is even greater.

With money in the bank, the players don't worry about their future as much as they once did. Articles which promote them are not that important any more. Such articles boost the ego but not the economics.

The writers have changed, too. They're still fans— just like the old-time writers—but they're not hero-worshipers. There is still a touch of that in most writers. The average guy covering a ball club played ball as a youngster, probably dreamed of being a pro. But once on the beat, he becomes disillusioned. His heroes are stripped of their larger-than-life qualities which he once attributed to them. Now they are just a bunch of ordinary people who sweat and bitch and cuss like anyone else.

The old-time writers wanted to be more a part of the gang. They socialized more with the players. They covered up for them. Babe Ruth was a heavy drinker and a womanizer. Nobody ever wrote that in the paper—at least not in a vicious sort of way. The late Tom Sheehan, who pitched for the Yankees and was close to Babe Ruth, once told me about a trip he and the Babe took from downtown to Yankee Stadium.

They took a cab in the late morning and headed for the game.

"As we went through upper Manhattan," Tom recalled, "the Babe told the cabbie to stop.

" 'I gotta girl waiting for me in this apartment house,' he told me. 'Tom, you stay here in the cab. I'll be back.'

"Fifteen minutes later, the Babe was back in the cab. He had completed his matinee romance and was ready for another kind of action—hitting home runs."

The New York writers ignored the Babe's goings-on, just as they overlooked the drinking problem which beset his teammate, pitcher Waite Hoyt. Waite eventually reached a point where he realized he had to quit drinking. He went into the hospital and when he came out, he never drank again.

The writers reported Hoyt's hospitalization as due to amnesia. This amused Waite's good friend and drinking companion, Babe Ruth. So, the Babe sent Hoyt a telegram:

"Read about your case of amnesia," it said. "Must be a new brand."

Paul Waner, one of baseball's great hitters, used to say that when he was drunk and at bat he would always pick the larger of the two baseballs to swing at.

Roy Parmelee, one-time big league pitcher, once told me that Paul Waner was the best hitter he pitched against.

"But Paul was a heavy drinker," Roy explained. "If he was drinking heavy before the game, he'd hit to left. Otherwise, as a left-handed hitter, he would pull the ball to right. So, we'd always send somebody over to talk with him before the game and find out just how drunk he was. Then, we'd know how to pitch to him."

Today Waner and the Babe would be in headlines with their peccadillos. But in their time, they were protected by a friendly press.

TV and radio have put pressure on the modern writer. The fan of today wants to know *why* things happened. The writer must visit the clubhouse after the game for quotes from the manager and the players. The old-timers—in pre-TV times—wrote their stories without leaving the press box. If there were opinions in the stories, they were those of the writer—not quotes from a clubhouse interview.

When I traveled with the New York Giants, Rud Rennie covered the games for the *New York Herald Tribune*. Ten or fifteen minutes after the game, Rud had written his story, filed it with the Western Union telegrapher and was in a cab headed back to the hotel. He probably never visited a clubhouse after a game in his entire career.

I think the writer today works a lot harder than his predecessors. He is also better educated and is more talented than the earlier writers. Today's writing is much more incisive and generally more literary than the stories I read when I was a youngster.

When I was growing up in Atlanta, the writers were my heroes. I worshiped them almost as much as I did the players. I read the nationally syndicated stars—Grantland Rice, Paul Gallico, Damon Runyan, and Westbrook Pegler—but my day-to-day diet came from the typewriters of Ed Danforth, Morgan Blake, and O. B. Keeler.

Keeler, because he had followed every step of Bobby Jones's career, was the most famous of our local writers. However, he also covered football, baseball, tennis, and even the opera.

When I began broadcasting, I was 22 years old. Keeler was in his late sixties. Despite the age difference, we became friends. "Pop," as everybody called him, was a heavy drinker. Once Bobby Jones and his wife, returning from a Chattanooga tourney, dropped an inebriated Keeler off at my radio station and asked me to escort him home. They were hurrying to a dinner date and didn't have time to get him settled.

Pop loved old books and mementos. I was living at my mother's house and really getting into collecting baseball guides, pictures, and other memorabilia. I invited Keeler to our home for dinner to view my collection. My mother, a great cook, worried and fussed over the dinner. We set the time for 6:30. She planned the dinner right to the minute. She baked a ham, made homemade biscuits, prepared the vegetables. Everything was ready at 6:30—everything but Keeler. He didn't show. We waited another hour.

"It's 7:30," my mother said, "shall we serve without him? Or shall we wait?"

"Let's wait another 30 minutes," I said.

At 8 p.m. Keeler still had not arrived. My mother shrugged her shoulders and began to put on the dinner for the rest of us.

Just then we heard a taxi in the driveway.

"Here he comes," I said.

I ran out the door to the taxi. Keeler was emerging from the cab. The instant I saw him, I knew he was drunk.

He stood in the driveway and beckoned to me.

"Ernie," he whispered, "I came by to tell you that I can't make it tonight."

Seeing how drunk he was and anticipating my mother's reaction, I heaved a sigh of relief.

"Thanks for letting me know, Pop," I told him. "We'll do it again some other time."

Another sports-writing hero of mine in Atlanta was Jimmy Jones. When Jones was the baseball writer for the *Constitution*, I was the 16-year-old Atlanta correspondent for *The Sporting News*. Often he would use my statistics in his stories. Later we were both in the Marines together and became good friends.

Jones led the league in absent-mindedness. One morning he was eating a late breakfast with his wife in a Macon, Georgia cafe. The boxer W. L. (Young) Stribling came to the door and Jimmy got up to meet him.

"Jimmy," said Stribling, "I'm flying my plane to Atlanta. Come on and go with me."

"Sure," said Jones. "I'll be happy to go."

They headed for the airport.

But Jones forgot to go back to the table and tell his wife he was leaving. She was stuck with the check and a great deal of time on her hands.

After Jones had left the *Constitution* to take a job in Richmond, I worked on the sports desk of the *Constitution*. I was there for six years while in high school and college. My main job was working on the copy desk, editing and writing headlines. Once in a while, I'd have a writing assignment.

I was paid absolutely nothing my first summer of work.

Ralph McGill, who later became the Pulitzer Prize-winning publisher of the paper, was sports editor.

"Harwell," he used to say, "I don't like a man work ing for nothing. Here's a voucher for your carfare." And he would write out a voucher for ten dollars. Later the paper paid me a dollar a day.

However, I wasn't the only one working for small wages. The *Constitution* had an agreement with the University of Georgia journalism school.

Through the agreement, the top two or three bright lights from the University's junior class in journalism interned at the paper all summer following their junior year. If their work was satisfactory, they would return after graduation and become full-time employees of the *Constitution* at $10 per week.

My career at the *Constitution* ended after my college days. I had wanted to follow a newspaper career, but in the final months of my senior year at Emory, there was no opening at the *Constitution* or at any other newspaper. Instead, I landed a job at radio station WSB,

Atlanta, in May of 1940. Except for four years in the U.S. Marines, I have been in radio ever since.

Yet, I've never lost my interest in newspapers and the people of the profession. I kept writing for *The Sporting News* throughout my radio-TV career. When J. G. Taylor Spink was the editor and publisher, I often wrote the column which appeared under his by-line.

The phone would ring and Spink would say: "Ernie, I need a column on the bean ball," or it might be "Send me a column right away on Hugh Casey."

Funny thing about Taylor was that he never left his office. But if you read his column, you'd think he was flying from one big league city to another every day. He had other ghosts writing for him. Dan Daniel in New York, Stan Baumgartner in Philadelphia, and the Dodger traveling secretary Harold Parrott were some of his contributors. Also, to further the on-the-scene concept, Taylor liked for his column to begin with some personal reference to him. It might go something like this:

"Jackie Robinson looked up at me from tying his shoelace and said: 'Taylor, I'm tired of these National League pitchers throwing at me.' "

Taylor was a great editor and a fantastic idea man. He was one of the last bastions of national personal journalism.

Lulu and I were with Taylor and his wife, Blanche, when they vacationed in Phoenix a year before he died. Even while on an oxygen machine, he'd be in his cottage at Camelback Inn, ripping through hundreds of newspapers and trade publications, siphoning off ideas for *The Sporting News*.

He was mercurial and volatile. He would love you

one day and castigate you the next. You never knew what the next phone call from Taylor Spink would bring. He was the world's greatest cusser and some of his feuds with sports figures are legend.

He was often very generous, but seldom allowed anyone to know of his generosity. Other times he could be downright stingy.

In the days when I broadcast for the Dodgers and the Giants, the press and radio gang would go to Taylor's golf club in Webster Groves, Missouri. We were always the guests of Taylor Spink. Often two or three foursomes would go, eat lunch, and tour the links. You can imagine that the cost must have been staggering with as many as 16 freeloaders showing up to enjoy the full treatment.

Taylor reveled in hosting us. He was always too busy to be at the club, but he would provide transportation and pick up the tab for the entire party.

However, one day a large group from the Giants went to Taylor's club. We finished our golf and the three foursomes sat down to lunch. Bill Roeder of the *New York World Telegram* was out of cigarettes. He asked the waiter for a pack of Chesterfields. He tried to pay the waiter.

"I can't take cash," the waiter told him. "It's against the club rules. You'll have to sign the tab for the Chesterfields."

Everything else had been signed for—the golf, caddie fees, the luncheon for all the golfers—so, Bill signed for the 35-cent pack of cigarettes.

That was his undoing with Spink. A month later Taylor saw the cigarettes listed on the tabs when the bills came to the office. Roeder was never again allowed on the course. Never again could he go to Webster Groves to play with our group of golfers. Taylor was more than happy to pay for the whole binge of golf, caddies, lunch, and transportation. But a pack of cigarettes. Never! That was Taylor Spink.

Spink wasn't the only big-time sportswriter who depended on ghost writers. Jimmy Powers of the *New York Daily News* often called on his staff to turn out material under his by-line. Arthur Suskind, one of our TV assistant directors, was a Powers column supplier. Jim McCulley, covering the Giants for the *News*, was another. All the six years I worked in New York, I never saw Powers at a baseball game. I don't think he ever came. But the same was true of the Scripps-Howard star sports columnist, Joe Williams.

It was Powers who prompted one of the classic announcements from the Ebbets Field PA announcer, Tex Rickard. Powers had waged a campaign for major league ball parks to keep the fans as informed as the radio-TV listeners.

"The guys who buy the tickets," he wrote, "have a right to know at least as much as the non-paying fan at home. The clubs should at least tell the people at the park why lineup changes have been made."

The very same afternoon after Powers's morning column, the Dodgers were playing the St. Louis Cards at Ebbets Field. The Cards blasted the Brooklyn starter, Preacher Roe. They scored five or six runs before manager Burt Shotton could get Roe out of the game and summon help from his bullpen. With his head down Roe trudged off the mound.

Tex Rickard, remembering the column by Jimmy

Powers, cleared his throat and announced: "Preacher Roe has done left the game because he don't feel good."

Dick Young was working for the *Daily News* in those days, too. He was a strong influence in baseball circles. Young was one of the sharpest and best-informed reporters I ever knew. When he covered the Dodgers, he didn't like their manger, Burt Shotton. If the Dodgers won, it was a home run by Reese or Snider. If they lost, Young would write: "Kindly ole Burt blew another one."

While covering the Giants, Barney Kremenko, writing for the *Journal American*, became even more involved with a manager and the game. It was mid-May, 1951, Forbes Field in Pittsburgh. On the second pitch of the game, Giant manager Leo Durocher got into a heated argument with the umpires and was ejected from the game. He came to the press box and sat down next to Kremenko. Leo began to give signs to the Giant third base coach, Herman Franks.

However, Franks was having difficulty spotting Durocher. He could see Kremenko clearly. So Leo asked Kremenko to give the steal sign—lifting a hand over his head. For two innings nothing happened. With one out, Bobby Thomson walked. Kremenko was nervous. He adjusted his glasses.

"You gave the signal," shouted Durocher.

"I didn't," Barney told him. "All I did was fix my glasses." Then he tried to erase the signal by rubbing his hands over his chest. Finally, Leo settled down. With a 2-2 count on Monte Irvin, the next batter, he said, "Give the signal." Kremenko did. Irvin struck out and Thomson was out trying to steal second. It might have been the only time in major league history that a writer participated in the running of a game.

It's always been difficult for players to understand the role of a writer and especially puzzling to players to see the same story by the same writer published in different newspapers as they travel from town-to-town.

One spring training, the Giants were traveling through Texas. Bill Roeder of the *World Telegram* had written a story about Clint Hartung. "Hartung, once destined for Cooperstown and the Hall of Fame, is just hanging on these days," the story said. "The potential super-star's talents are now concentrated on playing the pinball machine in various hotel lobbies on the Giant spring training trip through Texas."

As the Giants stopped to play an exhibition in five or six Texas towns, Hartung would see that story each day in each one of those places. Finally, he couldn't hold off any longer. He paid manager Leo Durocher a visit in Leo's office.

"Skipper," he said, "I keep seeing this damn story by Roeder in every paper. What's the fine for socking a sportswriter?"

In New York the competition was keen among the writers. Writing was sharp and incisive. When I went from New York to Baltimore, I found a drop in the quality of the sports pages. The younger, newer writers in Baltimore were talented, but at that time they were dominated by the older, staid, more established writers.

The three Baltimore sports editors were Jesse Linthicum of the *Morning Sun*, Paul Menton of the *Evening Sun*, and Rodger Pippen of the *News-Post*. Pippen was a collector of cats. He seldom ventured away from his home and was almost never at the ballpark. Menton was the most influential of the three. He had good contacts and was an official advisor to some of the sports franchises. But he was a deadly dull writer. Linthicum was the epitome of the old school of sportswriters—the group that grew up around the pool hall and was on speaking terms with the local "sports" who nickel-and-dimed their way through life shooting pool or bowling, or betting on baseball, football, and the races. Jesse was always at the race track. And no matter how cold the weather, he was always in shirtsleeves. He hated basketball.

On the opening night of each pro basketball season, Linthicum always wrote this lead: "The basketball season opens tonight. Ho hum."

Since the passing of the old guard in Baltimore, the city's sports reporting has vastly improved. The present-day reporters are as good as, if not better, than their peers around the major leagues.

When I made my Baltimore-to-Detroit switch, I came to a city with outstanding sports pages. The sportswriting and the photography in Detroit has always been great. After I saw the Tiger-Cub 1935 World Series in Chicago, I ordered all the Detroit papers by mail. I still remember the outstanding coverage of that Series.

The last two championship Tiger seasons (1968 and 1984) provided contrasts in coverage. In 1968, the newspapers were on strike for a large part of the season. The writers didn't come back until mid-August. Some of the players facetiously suggested that was the reason the Tigers won the pennant.

In 1984, the coverage was intense. The Tigers 35-5 start attracted national media attention and that in itself fanned the fires of local interest. When the Orioles came to Detroit for their first series, the papers published special baseball sections. Already the overkill had started.

"If it's this way when we haven't even played you guys, what will it be if we ever get into a real crucial series with you?" Scotty McGregor, the Oriole pitcher asked me.

The Tigers kept winning and the papers kept up their massive coverage. At playoff and World Series time another crop of special editions was harvested. After the Series, each paper put out a slick paperback book commemorating the Tiger championship.

The Tigers are lucky to have such media attention. But Detroit has always been that way. Great photographers and great writers for years have whetted the interest of baseball fans.

The excellent quality of Detroit sportswriting traces back to the days of H. G. Salsinger who started writing big league baseball before the fabled Grantland Rice, Westbrook Pegler, or Paul Gallico. And then outlasted all of them. Salsinger was a confidant of Frank Navin, the early Detroit owner, and American League president Ban Johnson. He had many contacts and was influential in baseball circles.

In his latter days, Salsinger was the reigning czar of the Detroit press box. He disliked radio (TV wasn't enough of a factor to concern him). When I first began to visit Tiger Stadium as an Oriole announcer, Salsinger was in failing health, but his influence was still strong around the park. Radio people were barred from the press box. There was no hospitality room or any other perks for them.

We were enjoying pre-game meals in other parks. But in Detroit, it was a cold hot dog and a warm bottle of

Coke sometime around the third inning. These were delivered in a brown paper bag by a kid from concessions who lowered the goods through the roof of our booth.

Salsinger was an excellent reporter and a prolific writer. He appeared often in *The Sporting News* and other publications. Current Detroit writers have followed that path. Several of them are nationally known.

Another testimonial to Detroit sportswriters is the way several have moved from the sports pages to columns of general interest. Doc Greene, Pete Waldmeir, and George Cantor are three journalistic stars who went that route. Some of today's sportswriters could make that move, too; but they prefer to stay in sports.

Media attention toward the Tigers comes from all sections of the papers. Baseball is page one on opening day and for any other special baseball event. The society pages and fashion sections join the parade. And even editorials are penned about the Tigers.

In recent years a constant war has been waged by the two Detroit newspapers—the *Free Press* and the *News*. They are close in circulation and each is battling to survive. Since the Tigers are always a hot story, they pour on the baseball ink. The Tigers are lucky to be the beneficiaries of this competition.

Sometimes, the media members even make headlines themselves. The two regular beat writers—Jim Hawkins of the *Free Press* and Watson Spoelstra of the *News*— were caught up in the famed Denny McLain drama in 1970. On April 1 that year McLain had been suspended by Commissioner Bowie Kuhn until July 1 for "his involvement in purported bookmaking activities in 1967." His return in July was a national event. A crowd of

53,863, the largest in nine years at Tiger Stadium, greeted Denny and cheered his every move. Denny lasted 5⅓ innings. When he left the game the Tigers were trailing, but they managed to win in extra innings.

However, the layoff had hurt McLain and he struggled through July and August. The big hurrah had died down and Denny was just another mediocre pitcher. He needed attention.

"I'm going to dump a bucket of water on the writers," he told pitcher Joe Niekro. The word got around. Teammates began to rib Denny about his promise. He had backed himself into a corner. Now, he had to follow up his promise or lose face.

About 5:30 the afternoon of the August 28 night game, Jim Hawkins strolled into the Tiger clubhouse.

"Hey, Jim," yelled Niekro. "Sit down a minute. I want to talk with you."

Hawkins pulled up a stool and sat facing Niekro, whose locker was next to McLain's. The filled water bucket—undetected by Hawkins—was on the floor. McLain quickly picked up the bucket and poured the water over Hawkins's head.

"It really didn't bother me," Hawkins admitted later. "I didn't like it, but I looked on it as a kind of joke."

Jim went to the press box and wrote three paragraphs about the incident for the *Free Press*'s first edition.

About two hours later, Watson Spoelstra, not realizing what had befallen Hawkins, wandered into the Tiger clubhouse. He got the same water treatment from McLain. Waddy went to the press box and phoned Tiger GM Jim Campbell to protest the incident. Campbell then called Hawkins.

"Did McLain dump water on you?" he asked.

"Yes."

"Why didn't you tell me?"

"It's over and done," said Hawkins. "I didn't really feel that it was any of your business."

"I'm making it my business," shouted Campbell.

Campbell suspended Denny for a period not to exceed thirty days and fined him at the rate of $500 a day.

McLain was the media's delight. He craved attention. If things were slow, he would create an incident. He was constantly giving out quotes, then denying them. He was always in the headlines.

Denny would have made the headlines in any era. But in Babe Ruth's time a great deal of his off-the-field antics would have been overlooked. The paternalistic writers of the 1920s probably would have treated the water-bucket incident as a lively joke and never bothered to report it.

13

I Believe in Miracles

BELIEVE IN MIRACLES—AT LEAST THREE OF THEM. These are all strictly personal and they all touched different areas of my life. One miracle saved my life. Another saved my career and the third might have been the most unbelievable of the three.

My first miracle happened during World War II. I was in the U. S. Marines, a member of the 59th Replacement Battalion. We were stationed at Camp LeJeune, North Carolina. This was April, 1944. The Allied forces in the Pacific had come up against stiff opposition. The Marines—along with the other service branches—were rushing replacements into that area. Losses were mounting.

Because of my writing experience, I was a clerk in the battalion headquarters. I did typing and also was the writer-editor of the battalion newspaper. Many of the members of my outfit were under-trained for combat. They had been brought back to line duty from various desk jobs. Yet, within a few days they were to be shipped out from Camp LeJeune for overseas duty.

We were scheduled to leave on Monday. Like many of the wives, Lulu was coming to Camp LeJeune to say good-bye. We would be able to spend that final weekend together in the Camp LeJeune Hostess House.

I was in the midst of my typing on Friday afternoon when the Top Sergeant came over to my desk.

"Harwell," he said, "here's an order concerning you."

"Me? What do you mean?"

"Headquarters on the Post has asked for two men with newspaper experience. They need men for the Camp LeJeune newspaper. You're one of them. And that means you'll be staying here and not shipping out with us."

I got my gear together and reported for duty at headquarters. When Lulu arrived from Atlanta for that final weekend, I had good news for her. Sure, I missed being with my friends in the 59th, but down deep I knew that danger had been postponed.

The 59th Replacement Battalion shipped overseas. Eighty percent lost their lives in the God-forsaken islands Saipan and Peleliu. A miracle had saved me. I stayed at headquarters at LeJeune. Later, I did go overseas as a Leatherneck magazine correspondent and eventually ended my overseas career in China.

Miracle number two happened in Baltimore. This one didn't save my life; but it did save my baseball broadcasting career.

In the mid-Fifties sponsors were much more sensitive than they are now. When Chesterfield sponsored the Giants' broadcast, the agency would not allow us to refer to Jack Lohrke by his well-known nickname of "Lucky." When the Giants played in Phoenix, in the shadow of Camelback Mountain, any reference to the mountain did not set well with Chesterfield. In Baltimore, the sensitivity was just as severe. In this case, it applied to a commercial spokesman switching from one brand to another. Baltimore was a bitter battleground for two local beers—National and Gunther. The two breweries were owned by the Hoffberger and Krieger families. These two families had intermarried, a condition which seemed to heighten the rivalry between the breweries.

I came to Baltimore in 1954 to broadcast baseball for National. The Gunther Brewing Company owned the rights to the football Colts. After two years, the National people acquired the football games, so I did both sports the final year of my three-year contract. In that final year, Gunther announced that it had won the Oriole broadcast rights from National. The brewery also stated that the National announcers (Chuck Thompson and I) would not be retained because of our strong identity with National.

I was now a lame-duck broadcaster. During that second half of the '56 season, Gunther began to contact other announcers about the Baltimore job. Names of prospective Oriole announcers were tossed around in the local sports sections. It was a foregone conclusion that I was on my way out.

Partly as a routine act and partly as a polite gesture in my direction, Gunther's New York agency sent a man to talk with me. He made an appointment through David Woods, who was representing me. We agreed to meet at noon at Woods's office on Charles Street and go to lunch.

The agency man was late. Dave and I waited. He arrived from New York at 12:40 p.m.

"Sorry I'm late," he said. "We won't have a lot of time to eat. Let's try some Chinese food. Is there a place near here?"

"Just a block down from the office," Woods told him. "The China Inn."

I had never been to the China Inn. I don't think Woods had either. A waiter seated us, and in several minutes came back to the table. Before he even asked about a drink or luncheon order he said: "Hey, you guys. I've got a petition here you've got to sign. We can't lose Ernie Harwell. We've got to keep him here. Gunther has to hire him to do the Oriole games."

You could have knocked me over with a chop stick. I'd never been in this restaurant and certainly didn't know the waiter. It would have seemed like a setup to the Gunther agency man, except that he was the one who asked about Chinese food. We didn't sign the petition but I'm sure the request by the waiter made a lasting impression on the agency man. He talked about it all through lunch.

He returned to New York and recommended that Gunther keep me as their Oriole announcer, despite previous association with their rivals, the National Brewing Company.

I did stay on for the next three years. All because of the Chinese waiter and his petition. In those three years, that waiter, Wally Lee, and I became close friends and I never forgot the way he worked a miracle.

My third miracle was a matter of money.

It happened in California in June 1979. My son Gray had moved to Anaheim Hills to conduct a campus ministry at UCLA-Irvine. Housing was expensive and Gray told me he was in a bind to keep up his payments. When I visited him, he told me that he needed $10,000.

"Gray," I told him, "I certainly don't have that kind of money. I don't know how I can get it. Let's pray about the situation and see what happens."

Thursday, June 9, was an off-day. After breakfast, I had a message to call Bill James, manager at radio station WJR, our flagship station for the Tiger broadcast.

"Ernie," he told me, "here at the station we've been reviewing some figures. We've come to the conclusion that the station is not paying you enough. We want to give you an extra $10,000 right now."

I gasped. "Did you say $10,000?"

"That's right," James answered. "You can get it when you come home at the end of the week."

Like most people I had negotiated hard at salary time. But this time, there was no battle. Just out of the blue, $10,000.

Three miracles: the one in North Carolina saved my life; the one in Baltimore saved my career; and the one in California saved my son's home.

Yes, I do believe in miracles!

14

Players: The Tough, The Special and The Great

AFTER YOU'VE BEEN AROUND BASEBALL FOR A while, it's inevitable that somebody will ask, "Who's the greatest player you've ever seen?"

My answer: "Willie Mays."

There is no doubt in my mind. Mays hit with consistency and power. He was an excellent base runner and base stealer. He played center field with the adroitness of a brilliant shortstop. He possessed a great love for the game and played it with a special spirit and verve.

I was broadcasting in the National League when the great Joe DiMaggio was ending his 13-year major league career. So, I never got to assess Joe on a day-to-day basis. Mays was making his debut in 1951, the same year DeMaggio bowed out.

I remember Willie from his very first game.

In March 1951, manager Leo Durocher, owner Horace Stoneham and other officials drove to Sanford, Florida to see the highly touted 19-year-old rookie Willie

Mays in action. That afternoon Willie banged out three hits, including a home run, and made two fine catches.

"One year in the minors," said Leon, "and he'll be in a Giant uniform. The kid is great!"

Along came the month of May. The Giants had started slowly. Outfielders Don Mueller and Bobby Thomson weren't hitting; Durocher was getting restless.

He went to Stoneham and asked for Willie Mays.

"But Leo," Horace told him, "we've got a problem with all those fans in Minneapolis. Willie's hitting .477 and making great catches. They love him. If we bring him up now, we'll antagonize those fans."

"To hell with 'em. We need help. Bring him up."

Stoneham acquiesced.

The Giants called Sioux City where the Minneapolis team was playing. They traced Willie to a movie theater. In the middle of the movie a sign flashed on the screen, "Willie Mays, call your hotel."

Mays hopped a train and headed for New York. The Giants placed ads in the Minneapolis papers to try to placate the local fans. Within two weeks the Giants' front office had received three letters from different young women in Minneapolis, each with a similar message: "Willie left his clothes here in my apartment. What shall I do with them?"

Willie reported to the Polo Grounds in New York, and the Giants whisked him immediately to Philadelphia where Durocher's Dandies were battling the Phils.

When Willie stepped into the batting cage, everything stopped. Immediately, he began to bang drives into the left and left-center field stands. We all knew he was headed for super-stardom.

Willie went without a hit in five trips in that first game. When the Giants left Philadelphia he still didn't have a hit in 12 times at bat. Mays was a scared 19-year-old, trying to figure out why he was in the big leagues. Monte Irvin sat by him on the train journey back to New York, trying to tell Willie that the hits would come.

The Giants' next game was at the Polo Grounds against Boston. Before the game Mays went into Durocher's office.

"Mr. Leo," he said, "I ain't gonna make it. I can't hit up here. Why don't you just send me back?"

"Never happen, Willie," was the manager's answer. "No matter what you do, I'm sticking with you. You're my center fielder. Now go out there and relax and play your game."

In the first inning of that game, May 28, Willie hit a Warren Spahn fastball over the left field roof for his first major league hit after 12 unsuccessful trips to the plate. He failed to hit in the next three games and was one for twenty-six. Against the Pirates on June 2, Willie went two for four and from then on had a successful season. He finished with a .274 average and won Rookie-of-the-Year honors.

Leo's faith paid off. Of course, Leo had the backing of Stoneham; but, nevertheless, a manager without Leo's strong convictions might have given up on the skinny 19-year-old and changed his whole career.

To me, Willie's fielding was even more spectacular than his hitting. Great speed and a strong arm enabled him to make catches I have never seen by any other player.

For instance, in Mays's rookie season of 1951 the Giants were playing the Pirates in Pittsburgh. Left-hand–hitting Rocky Nelson sliced a hard line drive to left-center. Mays, as usual, got a quick jump but as he ran toward left field, he realized he could not reach the line drive with his glove hand. So, he simply reached out with his bare hand, and while racing full speed, grabbed the line drive. It was the greatest catch I have ever seen.

The sensational catch retired the side and Mays and his teammates headed for the dugout. When Willie arrived, the other Giants were silent. It was strictly the cold-shoulder treatment.

Finally, the ebullient rookie couldn't stand it any longer. He walked the length of the dugout to Durocher.

"Skipper, Skipper," he said in his high, squeaky voice, "didn't you see that? I just made a great catch."

"You did?" said Leo, feigning nonchalance. "I didn't see it, Willie. Go out and do it again next inning."

He went out and did it many times. He won many games for Leo with his glove, his bat, and his baseball instincts.

Not only was Mays a great player, he also had one of the sharpest of baseball minds. In talking with Joe Falls of the *Detroit News*, Mays's old teammate Bill Rigney recalled Willie's savvy.

"I'm trying to steal the signs of all the catchers in the league," Rigney told Falls. "We're getting them from second base and I'm writing them down in a book. The first time Mays gets out there—the first time—he looks in and he sees the whole sequence . . . three fingers, two fingers, one finger, three, one, two, three. He comes back to the dugout and he gives me the whole thing in sequence—the exact order. He says they're using the first set of signs and he was absolutely right."

Willie Mays was a natural and everything came easy for him. Another of my favorite players, Clint (Scrap Iron) Courtney was just the opposite. The game was a struggle for Clint. But he met baseball and life face-to-face. Courtney didn't even look like a ballplayer. He looked more like Mr. Peepers with muscles.

His first big league season was 1951 with the Yankees. In his first spring training appearance, Clint was catching the established veteran Ed Lopat. Lopat didn't throw hard, but was crafty. He fooled the opposition with slow, tantalizing pitches.

After two or three pitches which hardly reached the plate, Courtney whipped off his mask and strutted toward the mound.

"What the hell are you doing, left-hander?" he growled. And the rookie catcher cussed out one of the cleverest veteran pitchers in the game.

Clint caught only one Yankee game that season and the next year had been banished to the St. Louis Browns. He had caught for Brownie manager Rogers Hornsby in the Texas League and idolized him.

Like Hornsby, Courtney never backed down. No matter the odds, he had confidence he could win. Often, he lost; but he didn't let defeat—or anything else—deter him.

He wore big, wire-rimmed glasses and his chin always jutted out past a large chaw of tobacco. At all times he looked as if he was challenging whoever or whatever happened to be around. Clint was the first major leaguer I saw wearing blue jeans. His wife used to pick him up at the games in an old Chevy truck.

In 1954 on a dreary, wet afternoon at Memorial Stadium in Baltimore, Clint participated in one of the strangest of all strikeouts. Certainly, it consumed more time than any other strikeout in baseball history. Courtney was batting against the White Sox's Harry Dorish in the bottom of the ninth. Playing in the rain, the White Sox led, 4–3. But the Orioles had the tying and winning runs on base. Jim Brideweser was on second and Jim Fridley was on first. Two were out.

Courtney was a tough little hitter and seldom fanned. He had struck out only twice during the first two-thirds of the season.

Now the rain was getting worse. Courtney stepped away from the plate. Umpire Jim Honochick looked at the skies. Only one more pitch was needed. All of a sudden a heavy thunderstorm broke loose.

"Time," yelled Honochick. Out came the ground crew with the tarp to cover the field. Nothing to do now but wait.

The two teams waited for an hour and seven minutes. Finally, the rain let up, the field was readied and play resumed. Courtney stepped to the plate. Two out, two on, the count was still three and two.

Dorish took his stretch and pitched. In came a fast ball just above the knees. It grabbed the outside corner. Courtney kept his bat on his shoulder.

Honochick thrust his right arm into the murky Baltimore sky.

"Y're out," he shouted.

The game was over. Courtney had fanned for the third time that season.

"Yeah," said Scrap Iron after the game, "I struck out. But it took him over an hour to get me."

When he played at Baltimore, I'd go to Pimlico race track with Courtney. He enjoyed the races, but bet with abandon. One afternoon he had lost big bets on the first seven races. In the last race he picked a real dark horse. Somehow, Clint's horse won and for one of the few times he went home a winner.

At Washington he was such a reckless card player that manager Cookie Lavagetto had to put a nickel limit on the game to protect Courtney from himself.

Whitey Herzog told about a time Clint involved himself in a table tennis match. "A Korean expert was putting on an exhibition at our hotel," Herzog said. "He was sensational. But Clint told us he thought he could beat the guy. He challenged the Korean and each put up $50.

"Clint didn't have a chance. The Korean beat him 21-0, 21-0. Clint probably still wasn't convinced that the Korean was a better table-tennis player."

Courtney was involved in one of the most bitter of baseball fights. It happened in 1953 in St. Louis. Clint upended Yankee shortstop Phil Rizzuto with a slide into second base. Billy Martin jumped on Courtney. Allie Reynolds started punching him and the entire Yankee team took him on before the other Browns could come to his rescue.

Clint and Martin were ejected and later fined. It was another example of how the battling little bulldog never gave up. He would not stay out of a controversy and no challenge ever went unanswered with Clint.

The writer Milt Richman, traveling with the Browns in spring training, 1952, found out about Courtney's competitiveness. Milt was standing on the train platform with a group of the Browns needling them about their lack of speed.

"Heck," he said, "I can beat anybody on this team in a foot race."

"Can't beat me," Courtney told him.

So, the course was staked out some hundred yards down the railroad track. Richman jumped into the lead and held on. In a last desperate surge, Courtney's legs went out from under him. He went sprawling into the cinders. His clothes were ripped, his arms, legs—even his face—embedded with cinders. Next morning he was stiff and could hardly walk.

Courtney went to Hornsby and confessed to the manager what had happened. He figured Rog would find out anyhow.

"Did you win?" Hornsby asked.

"I would have if I hadn't tripped."

"You're catching the whole game today. Maybe that'll smarten you up."

After his Brownie days, Clint bounced around. He went to Baltimore when the Browns shifted there in 1954, then to Washington, back to Baltimore and ended his playing career in Kansas City. By the time he'd reached Kansas City, I was broadcasting for the Tigers. Driving to the stadium one evening, I tuned in to Bob Elson, the Chicago announcer, interviewing Courtney.

"Scrap Iron," Bob said, "I'm a little surprised to see you here in Kansas City. For whom were you traded?"

"For a couple of rinky-dinks like myself," Clint answered.

Always a smart baseball man, Clint later became a manager. Paul Richards regarded him highly.

"Most people don't know," Paul pointed out, "just how much that little guy knows about baseball. All that pugnacious bluster fools 'em. If you watch him operate, you realize he knows what he's doing."

I don't think I ever met a player who was more of a competitor than Clint Courtney. Nobody wanted to win any more than old Scrap Iron. The irony of his life was that this rough, tough battler, who never backed down, died of a heart attack while playing Ping-Pong.

Other players can be as competitive as Courtney in quiet, unassuming ways. Alan Trammell, the Detroit Tiger shortstop, likes to win as much as the most heated competitor. Yet, he keeps his cool and is friendly and considerate.

I have broadcast for three teams which have won pennants—the Dodgers, Giants and Tigers. All three had outstanding shortstops. With the Dodgers it was Pee Wee Reese. Al Dark was the Giant shortstop. And the Tigers, since 1977, have marveled at the ability of Trammell.

All three of these players are favorites of mine. I could make a list why. All of them are:

Leaders

Gentlemen

Outstanding fielders

Smart base runners

Clutch hitters

All-around athletes

Men of high moral quality

Valid managerial material

Favorites of their managers

I think Sparky Anderson sees in Trammell the great infielder he hoped to be. He appreciates Alan's all-around ability and would rather have him at bat in a crucial situation than any other player on the Tiger team.

"Trammell is a complete major leaguer," says Anderson. "Taking into consideration his speed, power, defense, hitting, and instincts, right now he might be the best player in the game."

Such high praise reminds me of what Leo Durocher used to say about his Brooklyn shortstop Reese. And the way Leo, the Giant manager, used to rave about Alvin Dark. As enthusiastic and positive as he was, Leo could never match Sparky Anderson in a hyberbole-hurling contest. And Sparky is in his best form when the subject is Trammell.

"He is the man," says the Spark, "who has amazed me more than anyone. I always thought Dave Concepcion was untouchable. But when you take everything into consideration, we may be seeing someone even better than him. Alan is the most improved player over a five-year span in baseball. I have never seen a player get stronger and stronger, better and better and improve his mind the way Alan has done since I arrived in Detroit in 1979."

Comparing Tram with Reese and Dark, I have to take Trammell. My only reservation is that Alan is still only halfway through his career. Injuries have set him back at times and his physical condition could always be a threat. Reese played 16 years in the majors—all with the Dodgers. Dark was a major leaguer for 14 years. Alvin's first two seasons were with the Boston Braves. His next six-and-a-half he spent with the Giants. Then short stints with the Cards, Cubs, Phils, and Milwaukee Braves closed out his career.

Reese is in the Hall of Fame. Pee Wee's lifetime batting average was .269. He hit over .300 only once—he batted .309 in 1954. Dark's lifetime average was .289 and four times he hit .300 or better. I'd venture that in fielding ability Dark and Reese were even. Pee Wee had a big edge in base-stealing.

Now, let's examine Trammell's record. Alan's first season with the Tigers was 1977. He played only 19 games after coming up from Montgomery. Since then he has played seven full seasons. Out of those seven, he has hit .300 or better three times. His lifetime average entering the '85 season was .285. He has hit 14 homers in each of his last two seasons. (Dark's home run high was 23; Reese hit more than 14 homers only once—he had 16 in 1949.)

Alan stole 30 bases in 1984, his high. Reese's top total was also 30. Dark stole more than seven only once. He reached 12 steals in 1951. The two National Leaguers outdid Trammell in RBIs, both moving into the 80-plateau. Trammell's best RBI year was '84 when he knocked in 69 runners. However, Trammell should have another ten years in his career. I think that some season he will reach at least 90 RBIs.

Trammell is the best fielder of the three. He covers the most ground. He has the best arm.

All in all, Alan is a better shortstop than Reese and Dark. He is the Reese-Dark of the 1980s. If he can stay away from injuries, the rest of the baseball world will have the same high opinion of Alan Trammell that I do.

* * *

I've always felt the truest test of a leadoff man is: Would the opposing manager hate to see him lead off the ninth inning in a tie game? Willie Wilson of Kansas City would be an unwelcome sight leading off the ninth against you. Also, Bert Campaneris at the height of his career. But my number one choice over the years is Eddie Stanky.

Game after game, I watched Eddie lead off for the Giants in the early Fifties. He would reach base somehow. Sometimes he'd get a hit; other times, he would walk or maybe he'd be hit by a pitched ball.

Most leadoff men are supposed to be fast runners. They should be threats to steal. Stanky was slow. He never stole as many as 10 bases in any of his 11 big league seasons.

That was just one of the paradoxes of Eddie Stanky. He was a bundle of them. Nobody thought he was an outstanding player; but everybody wanted him on their team. All of us thought he would be an excellent manager, but his record in that department was mediocre. Off the field he was a true gentleman; on the field, he was a raging, do-or-die competitor.

Eddie's Brooklyn boss Branch Rickey was quoted as saying about him: "He can't hit, he can't run, he can't throw, but I'd rather have him on my team than any player I know."

Eddie was my pal. I was younger in those days when I covered the Giants and I was a part of the players' generation. Ed was two years older than I. On the trains, we often sat together, played cards, and insulted each other. His closest friend was Al Dark, another Southerner who was quite unlike Eddie. Alvin was much quieter, more reserved.

During the season, Stanky and I had a friendly one-dollar bet every day. Alternating days, one of us would try to pick three players not competing in a Giant game who would get a total of five hits among them. Sounds easy, but the odds are against it happening. The activity gave us something to talk about and kept us perusing the box scores.

Eddie liked to play golf, too. And I think it was on the golf course—even more than on the baseball diamond—that I saw his character emerge. One day we were playing at Bonnie Briar in Larchmont. On the first hole, Eddie hit his second shot near the out-of-bounds stakes. I had already hit my second shot down the fairway, so I went over to see where his ball was.

"Hey, that's close to the out-of-bounds," I said. "Could be either in or out.'

"Let's ask the caddy," he suggested.

"All right with me," I told him.

We called Stanky's caddy for a close look.

"What do you think, caddy?" asked Eddie.

"I don't know," he said.

"Looks either way to me," I told Stanky. "Call it whatever you think."

"No, the caddy should decide," Eddie said. "What about it, caddy? It's up to you."

"Mr. Stanky," the caddy said, "I shouldn't be making a ruling. Last week I told a lady she was out-of-bounds on this hole. She reported me to the pro and he gave me hell. I'll leave it up to you and Mr. Harwell."

After that statement, the caddy began walking down the fairway toward my ball. Stanky was livid. He picked up his ball and fired it toward the caddy. It breezed by the caddy's left ear and bounced down the fairway.

"I don't care what you call it," Stanky shouted at the caddy. "But show me some guts. Call it something."

No wonder they called him "The Brat."

Another Stanky nickname was "Muggsy" because he was a sort of modern John McGraw. I think that one was used only when he was playing with the Giants, where Mr. McGraw (always "Mr." among the Giant faithful) was a legend.

Eddie and I both lived in Westchester County when he played for the Giants. One afternoon near the end of the season we were riding home from the Polo Grounds. Eddie was speeding. A cop pulled him over and wrote a ticket. After the policeman finished his chore, Stanky held the ticket in front of the officer's face and tore the ticket into shreds.

"If you want me, you'll find me in Fair Hope, Alabama," he shouted at the cop. He gunned the car and sped away.

After losing games, he was a towel thrower and a stool kicker. I never understood such behavior and would chide him about it.

Some of Eddie's tantrums might have been for dramatic effect, yet the temper was always there smoldering and ready to erupt.

Like his idol, Durocher, Eddie hated umpires. He was nasty to them and they always returned the nastiness. One of his classic arguments was with Lon Warneke.

Eddie was the Cardinal manager. His pitchers were getting bombed and Eddie was getting more disgusted with each passing minute. He went to the mound to bring in another pitcher, his fourth of the game. He started to stall.

Warneke came out from behind the plate and told Stanky to stop stalling. Stanky ranted back at him. Words became heated. Finally Warneke said: "All right, Ed. That's enough. Who's your new pitcher?"

"It's gonna be Houdini," Stanky yelled. "Who did you think it would be?"

"Houdini?" asked Warneke, who knew the Cardinal roster, but was weak on the Who's Who among Magicians. "Houdini?"

"Yes, Houdini," repeated Stanky.

"Stanky," he said, "if that guy coming out of your bullpen right now ain't Houdini, you're out of the ball game!"

As a manager Eddie never finished higher than third. He reached that level twice with the Cards in four seasons. With the White Sox he finished fourth twice and ninth once. In 1977, his other managerial record was perfect. That year he managed the Texas Rangers for one game and won it.

On June 22, 1977, the Rangers fired their manager, Frank Lucchesi, and hired Stanky. Eddie had been away from big league managing for nine years. He was baseball coach at the University of South Alabama. He kissed his wife Dickie goodbye and reported for duty at Bloomington, Minnesota where the Rangers were playing the Twins a night game.

The Rangers won the game. Eddie went directly to his home hotel room and called Mrs. Stanky.

"I've had it. I've changed my mind. I'm coming home."

He never managed again.

* * *

During my 25 years of Tiger broadcasting, three players have grabbed the headlines and made them scream. No matter what these three did, they were news. Ron LeFlore started out in jail and became a Tiger; Denny McLain just about reversed that process; and Mark Fidrych, despite the premature ending of a potentially bright career, was the most charismatic of all the Tigers I watched.

McLain had come and gone before the other two arrived. He was cocky and sometimes sarcastic. I liked Denny and enjoyed being around him. I think most of his problems stemmed from his desire to conquer the whole world with one grandiose scheme. He was like a quarterback trying to throw the touchdown pass on every play. Eventually the odds had to catch up with him.

The Tigers knew they had a great prospect in Denny right from the start. In September 1963, Jim Campbell picked up Denny in Chicago and flew him to Washington where the Tigers were playing the Senators.

"We got to the park early," Campbell recalls. "Manager Charlie Dressen took Denny down to the bullpen to watch him throw. He came back and said, 'Jim, we've got one. We've caught lightning in a bottle.' "

That lightning didn't stay in the bottle. McLain's career was one storm after another. However, Denny seemed unperturbed by it all.

In the hectic 1968 season Campbell became fed up with all of Denny's doings outside of baseball. He summoned him to his office to investigate his involvement in a paint company venture.

"He was spending more time promoting the paint company than he was devoting to baseball," Campbell remembers. "He was on TV plugging the company, and going here and there all afternoon. I told him I was fed up with all that outside activity. I really chewed him out. McLain stood there in front of my desk and took it. Then he quietly walked out of my office. Suddenly, the door opened. It was Denny again. 'I like your style,' he told me. 'When my paint company becomes a success, I'll let you run it for me.' "

Denny had little sense of responsibility and felt that the rules were made for other people. I remember in 1967 he invited Ray and Carolyn Lane to his home for dinner. The Lanes showed up at the appointed time. Nobody was home at the McLain residence. Denny invited them again. Again, the same result.

"The first time," said Ray, "it wasn't too much of a shock. But the second time really baffled us."

In situations such as those, McLain would never apologize. He wouldn't even mention the incident. If somebody chastised him for his thoughtlessness or lack of manners, he would shrug his shoulders and say, "Well, forget it. It's no big deal anyway."

In 1968 when McLain won 31 games, he was the busiest player I've ever seen. Denny was appearing on all the national TV shows (including Ed Sullivan's), he was recording with his musical group on Capitol records, he was flying a plane, organizing a paint company, and building a sort of industrial empire.

"The only time I get to relax," he said, "is when I'm out there on the mound."

And Denny *was* relaxed on the mound. The Tigers always seemed to play well behind him. Maybe their defense was sharp because he worked quickly. But they also scored more runs for Denny than for any other pitcher.

In the '68 championship season, Denny seemed to have all the luck. His pitching partner, Mickey Lolich, had to struggle. Mickey won 17 games that year and was the hero of the World Series when he beat the Cards three times. Yet during the season, the fates were always kinder to Denny.

Incidentally, because of McLain, Lolich never received the recognition he deserved. Mickey was an outstanding pitcher. In 1971 he won 25 games for the Tigers, pitching 376 innings. For four straight seasons, he pitched over 300 innings.

In 1984 no pitcher in either major league pitched as many as 270 innings. Since 1977, only Steve Carlton of the Phillies and Jim Palmer of the Orioles have worked over 300 innings in a season.

Lolich never really liked McLain. He became very angry with him at the 1969 All-Star Game in Washington. Denny had flown Mickey and his wife Joyce to Washington from Detroit and had promised to fly them back. Denny pitched the fourth inning of that game. As soon as he had finished he went to the clubhouse, dressed, and took off—literally. The Lolichs were left stranded and had to get home on their own.

"Where were you? What happened?" Lolich asked McLain when he saw him back in Detroit.

"I had to leave," Denny told him. "Besides, Mickey, I'm not running any taxi company for you—or anybody else."

When Denny ran into deep trouble in Florida in 1984, none of his old teammates came forward to offer help. He had left too many stranded too many times.

Tiger fans alternated in their feelings between love and hate for McLain. He would praise them, then insult them. They reacted in kind. But once he began to win again, all would be forgiven.

In '68, Tom Aquino and I wrote a song about Denny. It was called "Maestro of the Mound":

The fans of Detroit didn't need him . . .
No more than a picnic needs rain.
And that's how the story gets started
Of near-sighted Denny McLain.
Denny yelled back when they booed him,
They said he'd never go far.
The fans tried to prove that he wouldn't
By putting a bomb in his car.

Chorus: Oh, Denny McLain, Denny McLain,
     There's never been any
     Like Denny McLain.

One lonely night at his organ
Denny selected his pitch.
This musical-man came up with a plan
To make him both famous and rich.
For a new look while playing in night clubs
His contact lenses were great.
And out on the mound, Denny soon found
He could now even see as far as the plate.

Chorus: Oh, Denny McLain, Denny McLain
     There's never been any
     Like Denny McLain.

His pitch on the organ was perfect,
And he never lost any chords.

With eyes 20–20, once near-sighted Denny
Won all of the baseball awards.
Yes, the fans of Detroit really love him.
Now they never complain.
All of their jeers have turned into cheers
For the Maestro, Denny McLain.

Oh, Denny McLain, Denny McLain,
There's never been any
Like Denny McLain.
Perfect rhythm, perfect pitch,
Perfect sight and sound . . .
There's never been any
Quite like our Denny,
The MAESTRO OF THE MOUND

Copyright 1968 Ravin Pub. (ASCAP)

Like McLain, Ron LeFlore wanted too much too
soon. He came from behind the prison walls, became
an overnight sensation as a Tiger, and then threw it
away. LeFlore's final year with the Tigers (1979) was
the first year that Sparky Anderson managed the team.

Sparky had a warning for LeFlore. "Ron," he told
him, "if you think that prison was tough, wait 'til you're
making the big dollars. That's real prison. It has been
true forever, Ron, that money is the root of all evil."

LeFlore's later actions proved Sparky's words pro-
phetic. In December 1979, the Tigers traded him to
Montreal. After a poor year there, he went to the White
Sox. Two troubled years with Chicago and Ron's prom-
ising career ended abruptly.

I was in on the start of the LeFlore story. In 1972

Lew Matlin, director of community affairs for the Tigers, and I discussed a trip to Jackson, Michigan prison. We wanted to take the Tigers' great pinch hitter Gates Brown to the prison and have a talk session with the inmates. At one time Gates had been confined to the reformatory at Mansfield, Ohio. We felt that the prisoners could relate to Gates and would enjoy hearing him. But when we couldn't get together with the prison officials on a date, we put off the idea until the next season.

In mid-May of 1973 we had it settled. Lew and I would take Gates to Jackson. Other Tigers would go with us. We got a promise from Aurelio Rodriguez, Willie Horton, and Frank Howard. A couple of days before our planned date of May 23, Brown hurt his leg. He couldn't go. Horton and Rodriguez backed out. Our ranks had been decimated.

The night before our trip, I was in manager Billy Martin's office telling him what had happened.

"Hey, I'll go with you," he said.

"I'll get Jimmy Butsacaris to take me. We'll meet you there."

Matlin, Frank Howard, and I left Tiger Stadium at 10 the next morning. We met Martin and Butsacaris at the prison. It was a cool, rainy day. But the prisoners came out into the yard and we put on a question and answer session for them.

One black prisoner shouted from the audience to Martin: "Billy, I hear there's a lot of dissension on the Tigers between the white guys and the blacks. How 'bout it?"

"Listen," Martin said. "Nothing to it. Willie Horton

and Frank Howard are roommates on the road. How'd you like to try and break into that room?''

After the session, we toured the prison. In the hospital, Martin met Ron LeFlore. Ron had been touted to Billy as the best baseball player in the prison. Several of the prisoners had spoken to Billy about him. Later we learned that Butsacaris had been getting letters for over a year about Ron.

"Mr. Martin, I'd like a chance with the Tigers," LeFlore said to Martin. "I know some of the guys have told you about me."

"Sure, sure," answered Billy. "We'll arrange for you to come up to Detroit and work out with us."

It's an old story. The prospect begs for a chance. The manager or some other official says, "Sure, we'll get you a tryout."

This time Martin followed through. LeFlore was near being paroled. He came to Tiger Stadium and put his wares on display. I was there. I saw him hit several drives in the stands. I saw his great running speed and his raw ability.

The Tigers liked what they saw. They asked Ron to come back after his prison discharge for another tryout at Butzel Field. They looked him over again and signed him on July 2, 1973.

By the end of the following season Ron LeFlore was on the major league Tiger team. He had five good years with the Tigers and led the league in stolen bases and runs scored in 1978. Then he began to decline.

Ron and Sparky Anderson never hit it off. Ron was never able to subject himself to Spark's discipline. LeFlore wanted to make it the easy way. Often he was late reporting to the stadium. He liked to talk big and strut around the clubhouse. It was evident he wouldn't last long under the Anderson regime. After he left the Tigers, he never regained his stature as a star although he stole 97 bases in 1980 at Montreal.

In his final year with the White Sox in 1982 Ron had numerous run-ins with manager Tony LaRussa. Le-Flore was suspended twice and in the last month appeared only as a pinch runner. Ron's second suspension came after narcotic officers had arrested him on September 30. Their search of his home allegedly uncovered drugs and firearms.

LeFlore has played no more baseball since that second suspension by the Sox. He was the number one sports story in Detroit at the zenith of his career. Jim Hawkins wrote a biography of him and Ron's rise from convict to major league star was depicted in a movie, based on that book. Ron—more than any other major-leaguer—should have known the consequences of going the wrong way. He had been there once and paid. Now, in his own way, he is paying again.

I had a special feeling for Ron. I was there when he was discovered. He was warm and friendly to me. He had visited my home and eaten dinner with my family. My heart ached when he blew his chance to become a very special kind of baseball hero.

The third Tiger headliner, Mark (The Bird) Fidrych was entirely different from LeFlore and McLain. He was an even bigger star than those ill-fated two.

Mark Steven Fidrych had been in the Tiger organization three years when spring training rolled around in 1976. He was not even on the Tigers' major league roster. But he became the sensation of the '76 season. Although he didn't make his first start until May 15, Mark went on to win 19 games that season. He was to win only ten more the rest of his career. But for that one year he was a national hero . . . a fresh breeze for the fetid atmosphere of salary battles, court suits, lawyers, agents, and accountants.

There are several ways to judge a player. But the best way to assess him is by the reaction of his teammates. With the Tiger players, Fidrych was tops. They loved him—just as the fans loved him. Mark was flaky. He talked to the ball, jumped in the air, and went around the diamond shaking hands with his teammates—but he also produced. And the Tiger players admired him. They quickly accepted him. He gave his teammates credit for his success and they appreciated his thoughtfulness and generosity.

Players on the opposing teams admired him, too. Often when he took curtain calls after a victory, players on the other team would stay in their dugout to watch. I think Mark was the first big-leaguer to take a curtain call on a regular basis.

Wherever he pitched he drew big crowds. The rival club owners would pray that Fidrych's pitching turn would come during their series with the Tigers. He was extra money in the bank for everybody.

He was great because he was natural. Bill Veeck told me, "If someone had tried to stage Fidrych, it would have fallen flat. It would have been artificial."

Ralph Houk was the Detroit manager that year. He handled Fidrych well. He kept him under wraps for the first six weeks of the season. An early disaster might have been the introduction to a different story. Anyway, you can't argue with success. Houk made the right move.

The kid had excellent baseball instincts. The first two times he handled run-downs, he followed the fundamentals with clinical perfection. Off the field, he was easy and natural with the media and with the fans.

He had a delightful way of expressing himself, sprinkling his conversation with one malaprop after another. Early in that first year, Houk had to move The Bird to the far end of the dugout to avoid eardrum damage from Mark's constant cheerleading. Once during a rally, Fidrych shouted, "Come on, gang. Remember a hit is as good as a walk."

Later when Mickey Stanley was thrown out attempting to steal third base, Fidrych yelled, "All right, team, let's capitalize on that now."

We were in Oakland in September when I saw an item in a syndicated entertainment column that Fidrych would appear in a baseball TV series. I asked him about it. "I don't know," he said. "Maybe my agent will be making a deal. But I'll tell you this, Ernie. No matter what happens, I'll have the last hear-say."

Another time we were on the team bus headed down Michigan Boulevard, in Chicago. It was the summer that the King Tut exhibition had been on display at the Chicago Art Institute. Much publicity had surrounded the event. Several of the players were talking about the news items and the long lines of people who were anxious to see the King Tut artifacts.

Overhearing the conversation, Fidrych turned around and asked, "King Tut? What is that, a new rock group?"

Poor Bird. He was a one-year sensation. He hurt his

knee in spring training of 1977, then got arm miseries and never was able to reach those heights again. He tried. He tried as much as anybody ever tried. Therapy, operations, rehabilitation—all of it.

The Tigers finally gave up on him and released him after the 1981 season. The Red Sox signed him the next February, but he never again recaptured his glory.

The greatest quality Mark Fidrych showed me was this: up or down, on top or on the bottom, he was still the same, great enthusiastic kid.

He was baseball's answer to the challenge put forth by Rudyard Kipling in his poem "If":

"If you can meet with Triumph and Disaster
And treat those two imposters just the same . . .
Yours is the Earth and everything that's in it.
And—which is more—you'll be a Man, my son."

The player who earns my vote as the greatest ballplayer of all time never learned to accept defeat with equanimity. But that was one of the few qualities Tyrus Raymond Cobb lacked.

Willie Mays was the greatest player I ever saw in action. But I have no doubt that even wondrous Willie would have to take a back seat to the Georgia Peach.

I never saw Cobb play, but I did get to know him in his later years. My first meeting with him was in his home town, Royston, Georgia, in 1941.

"Cobb's come back to Royston," I told Mark Bartlett, the program director at WSB. "Let me have an engineer and I'll get an interview with him."

"Cobb will never talk to you," Mark said. "He's a

bitter, mean old man. He'll have nothing to do with you."

I found out differently. We drove the 120 miles to Royston and met the Great Man in the late morning. He was most cordial. A drink or two had already warmed him up for me. And he talked. The problem was not getting him to talk, but getting him to stop talking. My entire 15-minute show was Ty Cobb and we almost ran overtime.

Later I was with him several times at the Masters golf tournament in Augusta. And I also had a pleasant visit with him at an Old-Timers' game in Baltimore.

At Augusta, Cobb told me a story which I wrote for the *Saturday Evening Post*. It was my first contribution to a major magazine. The story involved another of my early heroes, Grantland Rice.

In the summer of 1904, Rice was sports editor of the *Atlanta Journal*. He began to receive anonymous telegrams from Anniston, Alabama. Each shouted high praise for a local player named Ty Cobb. Rice kept tossing the wires into a wastebasket, but finally his resistance broke down. He took a train to Anniston to judge for himself.

What he saw left no doubt as to Cobb's potential. The youngster collected five hits and stole home to assure Anniston a victory. Rice headed for the local telegraph and filed a 300-word dispatch to his paper.

He wrote: "Ty Cobb was a comet with a fiery tail here this afternoon. He blazed the Annistons to victory with his bat and base running. Here is a young man who someday may make his mark in the baseball world."

Even though Rice was now sold on the phenom, the

anonymous wires continued and the *Journal* printed them with regularity. Cobb was always grateful to Rice for helping him in his start. Not until years later did he admit to Rice that the anonymous Anniston correspondent was Cobb himself.

There are many stories about Cobb's desire to succeed. Mike Kinney, who was a Tiger batboy in the Cobb era, told me one.

"I worked in a butcher shop near Navin Field," Mike said. "Mrs. Cobb was going to have company, so she ordered a roast. I delivered it. Nobody was home so I put the meat inside the screen door. When Ty and Mrs. Cobb came home they found that the meat had spoiled. Ty went straight to the butcher shop and had a vicious fistfight with the butcher."

Fred Lieb, the New York baseball writer, followed Cobb's diamond exploits for twenty years and also knew him for many years after Ty retired. Fred related this story about Cobb:

"Ty was seated on the porch of a hunting lodge in Georgia when a dog came up the steps and lay down on the porch. He kicked the dog and sent him sprawling down the steps and into the yard. 'Damn dumb dog,' Ty shouted. 'You don't belong on this porch. You're not a house dog. You're a yard dog. Get on down there where you belong.' "

Another man who knew Cobb well was Nap Rucker. Nap was Ty's roommate when they were both with Augusta. Later Rucker became a fine pitcher for the Brooklyn Dodgers. When I knew him he was a scout. In the days when Cobb and Rucker roomed together, there were no showers at the ball park. The players did not bathe until they returned to their boarding house.

One afternoon Rucker had been knocked from the mound and returned to the room ahead of Cobb. He undressed and slipped into a tub of warm water. A few minutes later, Cobb came in. He shouted and rapped on the door of the bathroom. Rucker, still dripping, came out.

Cobb screamed at him. Waving his arms wildly, he kept shouting: "I take my bath first! I take my bath first!"

Rucker was stunned. "What's the matter with you?" he asked. "Have you gone crazy?"

Cobb became calmer. He shrugged. "Nap, try to understand. I got sore when you beat me to the bathtub. I've got to be first—no matter what it is."

Throughout his career Cobb was first. He made himself baseball's greatest. It was fitting that he was the first player to be elected to the Baseball Hall of Fame.

Death finally stopped him. Ty died July 17, 1961 at Emory University Hospital in Atlanta, at the age of 74. That same night the Tigers—Ty's old team—played a game at Tiger Stadium. Jim Campbell asked me to write a eulogy for use on the public address system. Here is what I wrote for Joe Gentile, the PA man, to read:

"Baseball's greatest player—Tyrus Raymond Cobb—died today in his native Georgia. Cobb was genius in spikes. His mind was the keenest ever to solve the strategy of the diamond. He was fiery and dazzling on the base paths. For 24 years of high-tensioned baseball action, his name led all the rest. He was the best—in hitting, base-stealing, run-making—in everything.

"Cobb's rise to fame in the early 1900s kept step

with the progress of baseball as a national spectacle. His dynamic spirit was a symbol for the ever-growing industrial community he represented—Detroit, Michigan.

"And now, here in a baseball stadium where the cheers were the loudest and longest for this greatest of all Tigers, let us stand and pay final tribute to him in a moment of respectful silence."

The crowd stood in final tribute to the genius from Georgia. Ty Cobb was the greatest of them all.

15

Signing Off

THE QUESTION I AM ASKED THE MOST IS: "HOW DID it feel when you made the Baseball Hall of Fame?" I tried to answer that question in the speech I made at Cooperstown the day I was inducted into the Hall. Ralph Kiner had announced that I had been given the Ford C. Frick award for my contribution to baseball, and this is the way I responded that day, August 2, 1981:

Thank you, Ralph, and thank you, folks, for that warm Cooperstown welcome. This is an award I will certainly cherish forever.

I praise the Lord here today and I know all my talent and all my ability come from Him and without Him, I am nothing. And I thank Him for His great blessing.

I'd like for you to meet my very best friend. She's my best friend, despite the fact that this month we celebrate our 40th wedding anniversary—Lulu Harwell.

My son Bill, his wife Dianne and their youngsters. My son Gray, his wife Sandy and their three youngsters. And my daughters, Julie and Carolyn. I'm very proud of this award, but I'm even more proud of my family.

You know, the life and times of Ernie Harwell can be capsuled in two famous quotations—one from a left-handed New York Yankee pitcher and the other from a right-handed English poet. The Yankee pitcher, Lefty Gomez, once said: "I'd rather be lucky than good." And the poet, Alfred Lord Tennyson, once wrote in his epic poem "Ulysses," "I am a part of all that I have met."

Well, I know that I'm a lot luckier than I'm good. I've been lucky enough to broadcast some great events and to broadcast the exploits of some great players. When I went to Brooklyn in 1949, Jackie Robinson was at the height of his brilliant career. With the Giants I broadcast the debut of Hall-of-Famer Willie Mays. When I went to Baltimore, the great Brooks Robinson came along to replace my good friend George Kell at third base. And in my 22 years at Detroit, it's been a distinct privilege to watch the day-by-day consistency of Hall-of-Famer Al Kaline.

Yes, I'm lucky that I've been there and I've been at some events, too. I want to tell you about one that Ralph mentioned—Bobby Thomson's home run, October 3, 1951. I felt a little sorry for my Giant broadcasting partner, Russ Hodges that day. Ole Russ was going to be stuck on radio. There were five radio broadcasts. I was going to be on coast-to-coast TV and I thought I had the plum assignment. Well, as you remember, it turned out quite differently.

Russ Hodges's record became the most famous sports

broadcast of all times. Television had no instant replay, no recording in those days. Only Mrs. Harwell knows that I did the telecast of Bobby Thomson's home run. When I got home that night after the telecast, she said to me, "You know, Ernie, when they turned the camera on you after that home run, I saw you with that stunned look on your face. And the only other time I'd ever seen it was when we were married and when the kids were born."

That other saying . . . "I am a part of all that I have met." I think that would have to begin with my wonderful parents back in Atlanta. When I was a youngster five years old I was tongue-tied. They didn't have much money, but they spent what they had sending me to speech teachers to overcome that handicap. I know a lot of you people who've heard me on the radio still think I'm tongue-tied. But, through the grace of God, officially I'm not tongue-tied anymore.

Also, I am a part of the people that I've worked with in baseball who have been so good to me. Mr. Earl Mann of Atlanta, who gave me my first baseball broadcasting job; Mr. Branch Rickey at Brooklyn; Mr. Horace Stoneham of the Giants; Mr. Jerry Hoffberger in Baltimore; and my present bosses, two of the greatest ever, Mr. John Fetzer and Mr. Jim Campbell.

I'm also a part of the partners that I've worked with . . . and there have been so many great ones, beginning with Red Barber and Connie Desmond at Brooklyn and continuing to my present partner, WJR's Paul Carey.

But, most of all, I'm a part of all of you people out there who have listened to me, especially you people in Michigan—you Tiger fans. You've given me so much warmth, so much affection and so much love. I know that this is an award that is supposed to be for my contribution to baseball. But let me say this: I have given a lot less to baseball than it's given to me. And the greatest gift that I've received from baseball is the way that the people in the game have responded to me with their warmth and their friendship.

Yes, it's better to be lucky than good. And I'm glad that I'm a part of all that I have met.

We are all here with a common bond today. We're all here because we love baseball.

Back in 1955 (Ralph referred to this) I sat down and wrote a little definition of baseball to express my feelings about this greatest game of all. I know that a lot of things have changed about the game since then—especially in this strike-torn and strife-filled year. But my feelings about the game are still the same as they were back then, and I think maybe yours are too.

And I'd like to close out my remarks for the next couple of minutes (with your indulgence) to see if your definition of baseball agrees with mine:

Baseball is the President tossing out the first ball of the season. And a scrubby schoolboy playing catch with his dad on a Mississippi farm.

A tall, thin old man waving a scorecard from the corner of his dugout—that's baseball. So is the big, fat guy with a bulbous nose running home one of his 714 home runs.

There's a man in Mobile who remembers that Honus Wagner hit a triple in Pittsburgh 46 years ago—that's baseball. And so is the scout reporting that a 16-year-old sandlot pitcher in Cheyenne is the coming Walter Johnson.

Baseball is a spirited race of man against man, reflex against reflex. A game of inches. Every skill is measured. Every heroic, every failing is seen and cheered—or booed. And then becomes a statistic.

In baseball, democracy shines its clearest. The only race that matters is the race to the bag. The creed is the rule book. And color, merely something to distinguish one team's uniform from another's.

Baseball is a rookie (his experience no bigger than the lump in his throat) as he begins fulfillment of his dream. It's a veteran too—a tired old man of 35 hoping those aching muscles can pull him through another sweltering August and September.

Nicknames are baseball. Names like Zeke and Pie and Kiki, and Home Run and Cracker and Dizzy and Dazzy.

Baseball is the clear, cool eyes of Rogers Hornsby; the flashing spikes of a Ty Cobb; and an over-aged pixie named Rabbit Maranville.

Baseball? Just a game—as simple as a ball and bat. And yet, as complex as the American spirit it symbolizes. A sport, business and sometimes almost even a religion.

Why, the fairy tale of Willie Mays making a brilliant World Series catch and then dashing off to play stickball in the streets with his teenage pals—that's baseball. So is the husky voice of a doomed Lou Gehrig saying: "I consider myself the luckiest man on the face of this Earth."

Baseball is cigar smoke, hot-roasted peanuts, *The Sporting News*, Ladies Day, Down in Front, "Take

Me Out to the Ball Game,'' and ''The Star-Spangled Banner.''

Baseball is a tongue-tied kid from Georgia growing up to be an announcer and praising the Lord for showing him the way to Cooperstown. This is a game for America. Still a game for America—this baseball!

Thank you.

Index

233

About the Author

Born in Washington, Georgia in 1918, Ernie Harwell started his career in baseball at age 16 as the Atlanta correspondent for *The Sporting News*. He broke into broadcasting as sports director of WSB-Atlanta in 1940 and went on to do play-by-play for the Atlanta Crackers, the Brooklyn Dodgers, the New York Giants, the Baltimore Orioles, and the Detroit Tigers. On August 2, 1981, Ernie Harwell was inducted into the Baseball Hall of Fame, receiving the Ford C. Frick Award for excellence in baseball broadcasting. He is celebrating his 30th year as the voice of the Tigers on WJR-Detroit, but his talents and accomplishments aren't limited to the broadcast booth. Read Lulu Harwell's delightful Foreword to TUNED TO BASEBALL to find out more.